AMERICA'S CHILDREN
WHO CARES?

AMERICA'S CHILDREN WHO CARES?

Growing Needs and Declining Assistance in the Reagan Era

Madeleine H. Kimmich

The Changing Domestic Priorities Series

John L. Palmer and Isabel V. Sawhill, Editors

THE URBAN INSTITUTE PRESS · WASHINGTON, D.C.

Library of Congress Cataloging in Publication Data

Kimmich, Madeleine H. 1950–
  America's children.

  (The Changing domestic priorities series)
  1. Child welfare—United States. 2. Federal aid to
child welfare—United States. 3. Family policy—United
States. 4. Welfare recipients—United States.
5. Intergovernmental fiscal relations—United States.
I. Title. II. Series.
HV741.K495 1985   362.7′95′0973   85-11114
ISBN 0-87766-386-6 (pbk.)

Printed in the United States of America

9 8 7 6 5 4 3 2 1

Design and front cover photograph by Francesca Moghari.
Other photographs by Babette Augustin (courtesy of *Potomac Almanac*).

THE URBAN INSTITUTE is a nonprofit policy research and educational organization established in Washington, D.C., in 1968. Its staff investigates the social and economic problems confronting the nation and government policies and programs designed to alleviate such problems. The Institute disseminates significant findings of its research through the publications program of its Press. The Institute has two goals for work in each of its research areas: to help shape thinking about societal problems and efforts to solve them, and to improve government decisions and performance by providing better information and analytic tools.

Through work that ranges from broad conceptual studies to administrative and technical assistance, Institute researchers contribute to the stock of knowledge available to public officials and to private individuals and groups concerned with formulating and implementing more efficient and effective government policy.

Conclusions or opinions expressed in Institute publications are those of the authors and do not necessarily reflect the views of other staff members, officers or trustees of the Institute, advisory groups, or any organizations that provide financial support to the Institute.

Listed below are the titles available, or soon to be available, in the Changing Domestic Priorities Series

Conference Volumes

THE SOCIAL CONTRACT REVISITED
Aims and Outcomes of President Reagan's Social Welfare Policy (1984),
edited by D. Lee Bawden

NATURAL RESOURCES AND THE ENVIRONMENT
The Reagan Approach (1984), edited by Paul R. Portney

FEDERAL BUDGET POLICY IN THE 1980s (1984), edited by
Gregory B. Mills and John L. Palmer

THE REAGAN REGULATORY STRATEGY
An Assessment (1984), edited by George C. Eads and Michael Fix

THE LEGACY OF REAGANOMICS
Prospects for Long-term Growth (1984), edited by Charles R. Hulten and
Isabel V. Sawhill

THE REAGAN PRESIDENCY AND THE GOVERNING OF AMERICA
(1984), edited by Lester M. Salamon and Michael S. Lund

CONTENTS

TABLES

FOREWORD

This book is part of The Urban Institute's Changing Domestic Priorities project. The project is examining changes that are occurring in the nation's domestic policies under the Reagan administration and is analyzing the effects of those changes on people, places, and institutions.

The Reagan administration has consistently sought to cut federal spending for the major programs providing services and income support to children and their families. Large reductions were enacted in fiscal 1982, although Congress rejected most of the proposed cuts for fiscal years 1983, 1984, and 1985. The programs most affected have been aid to families with dependent children (AFDC), medicaid, food stamps, and the social services block grant. State and local governments administer these programs and, except in the case of food stamps, also share financial responsibility. They, in turn, often rely upon nonprofit agencies for the actual delivery of some services. Thus any examination of the consequences of the federal cutbacks in programs providing services to children and their families must focus on the responses and adjustments made by lower levels of government and local agencies and how these have affected recipients.

Based on detailed empirical information from the relevant state and local agencies, this report by Madeleine H. Kimmich analyzes the behavior of state and local government in coping with federal cutbacks and the impact of public actions on nonprofit service providers. She also offers a useful perspective on how the recipients of assistance from these agencies have been affected by public policy decisions and how they have fared in the context of an eroding social support system.

The federal deficit continues to grow, prompting continued pressure on social spending. More changes in social services, health services, education services, and employment services are being considered by federal and state policymakers. This thorough examination of services to children and their families is important background for future decision making during this era of rethinking of public goals and purposes.

John L. Palmer
Isabel V. Sawhill
Editors
Changing Domestic Priorities Series

ACKNOWLEDGMENTS

The research for this book was supported by the Carnegie Corporation of New York under the auspices of The Urban Institute's Changing Domestic Priorities project. The report draws particularly from two Urban Institute studies: the Fiscal Limitations study under Department of Health and Human Services contract HEW-100-79-0174; and the Nonprofit Sector project, the relevant portion of which was supported by the Foundation for Child Development.

I thank my Urban Institute colleagues Eugene C. Durman, Demetra Smith Nightingale, Karen Pittman, Margaret Simms, and especially Jeffrey Koshel for their support and constructive criticism. Marleen Clark, a long-time friend and colleague, also offered helpful comments and encouragement. I only wish space permitted me to acknowledge the help I have received from many state and local child welfare officials who contributed to the Social Services Research Center projects upon which this book relies. At The Urban Institute Karen Wirt very competently edited the manuscript, which was typed and prepared for keyboarding by Marla Taylor and Mykki Jones.

ABOUT THE AUTHOR

Madeleine H. Kimmich is a former research associate in The Urban Institute's Social Services Research Center, where she specialized in human services programs for children, adolescents, and the elderly. She holds master's and doctoral degrees in social welfare policy from the University of California-Berkeley. She currently works in the Washington, D.C., area as a research consultant in data management and program evaluation.

CHAPTER 1

OVERVIEW

Children in the United States are born dependent like all other children of the world. Their basic needs must be provided by others—family, friends neighbors, older children, or service workers assigned by government or private social organizations. While children's dependency is biological fact, fundamentally nonnegotiable in the early years of a child's life, society's responses to the needs of children vary according to changes in political, social, and economic priorities. This book documents such a period of change in U.S. public policy, and the marked decline in the degree to which American society takes collective responsibility for the dependency of the nation's children.

In the 1960s and 1970s the United States government steadily expanded its role in maintaining America's children. Programs were established to assure children adequate nutrition, housing, and health care as well as protection against neglect and abuse. Also in that period federal policymakers defined children's needs to include social and economic development, and provided support such as special education, day care, recreation, job training. Many of these initiatives were in response to disturbing demographic trends that showed increasing numbers of children living in poverty, and a rapidly growing poverty class of female-headed families with children.

In 1981 more than 20 percent of all children in the United States lived in poverty; among black children the proportion was 47 percent. That year President Reagan signed into law the Omnibus Budget Reconciliation Act of 1981, milestone legislation that transferred much of the federal responsibility for the financing and setting of policy in social programs to state and local governments and to the private sector. The ensuing contraction of the federal role in children's services catalyzed myriad changes in the service delivery systems of state and local governments and the nonprofit sector, and in the opportunities for children and their families to receive services.

Subsequent initiatives by the Reagan administration suggest that

1

children's services will be under pressure for the rest of the decade, as the federal government seeks further spending cuts to reduce budget deficits. The president's 1985 budget included significant cuts in children's programs, specifically education for the handicapped, a proposed combined social services and community services block grant, summer youth employment, runaway and homeless youth, food stamps, child nutrition, aid to families with dependent children (AFDC), and medicaid; the 1985 budget also proposed elimination of all juvenile justice and delinquency prevention and legal services programs. Further cuts are proposed for 1986 in medicaid, AFDC, child nutrition programs, summer youth employment, and child abuse prevention; a freeze on funding for the social services block grant, child welfare services, runaway and homeless youth programs, Head Start, programs relating to the Job Training Partnership Act, Chapter 1 compensatory education, programs of the All Handicapped Children Act and the maternal and child health block grant; and elimination of the juvenile justice and delinquency prevention programs, Job Corps, and the work incentive programs for AFDC recipients. All of these changes challenge agencies' abilities to meet the future needs of children and their families.

This book looks at how the changes in funding have affected the provision of services for children during the first term of the Reagan administration. Has the gap between children's needs and provision of services widened? Has the risk increased that the needs will not be met? To answer these questions, the volume explores federal, state, and local changes in the policies and practices of selected programs affecting children and the implications of the changes for delivery of services. In addition to examining budgetary changes and demographic shifts, the discussion examines service delivery in various communities in the United States. Although not statistically representative of the nation, the findings derived from these community studies are useful in conveying an understanding of the practical implications of changes in budget figures or population trends.

After describing the nature of the problem during the 1981–84 period, the volume then investigates the changes that state and local governments have made to cope with the federal cutbacks and the national recession, with a particular focus on social services and health services, the areas in which programs are most clearly targeted on children. The nonprofit sector, government's partner in service delivery, is the next point of discussion—how it has responded to the decreasing public revenues and the growing demand for its public services. The last chapters address the implications and draw together the findings from all components of the analysis.[1]

The National Picture

The newly established House Select Committee on Children, Youth, and Families conducted a study of children and their needs that conveys a picture of dire economic circumstances of many children in the United States, particularly minority children and those living in households with female heads.

The findings of that study confirm that a smaller proportion of children received aid to families with dependent children (AFDC) in 1981 than in 1980 even though the poverty rate among families with female heads was rising. Federal outlays for twenty-five programs affecting children—social services, health, nutrition, education, employment, and income support—decreased by 11 percent between fiscal years 1981 and 1984, after adjusting for inflation. Particularly hard hit were youth training programs (part of the Comprehensive Employment and Training Act of 1973), child nutrition programs (including school lunches and breakfasts, child care, and summer feeding programs), food stamps, most social service programs affecting children, the preventive health services block grant, and AFDC.

Restrictions on federal funding were generally imposed in two ways: as direct reductions in grant programs (often accompanying a shift from service-specific grants to a block grant), or as changes in eligibility criteria or service coverage in entitlement programs. The entitlement programs are the mainstays of the support system for the poor: AFDC, medicaid, child nutrition programs, and food stamps. Changes in the design of these programs potentially have the most far-reaching effects on children and their families.

Insofar as federal funds are but one of a number of sources that state and local governments draw upon to provide services to children, it is important to place in proper perspective the potential impact of

1. The material presented in this volume draws on the findings of four Urban Institute studies conducted from 1981 to 1984. Two studies are of the impact of federal grant-in-aid programs—one focuses on child welfare services in six states, the other examines all human service programs in eighteen states. The third assesses the impact of recent changes in federal social policy on four communities: Boston, Detroit, San Diego, and Richmond, Virginia. The fourth study examines the nonprofit agencies that primarily serve children and youth and how those agencies have been affected by recent changes in human services policy. More detail on these studies is provided in the appendix.

reductions in federal expenditures for children's services. For example, employment and training programs tend to be largely federally funded, while the federal role differs widely in the social services offered in various states and localities. It is the rare community, however, that is untouched by changes in federal social welfare policy, even in a single program area. The question then arises, how have local public authorities responded to the federal retrenchment?

State and Local Government Response

The early 1980s witnessed many significant changes in state and local provision of children's services. Federal revenue reductions, coupled with a recession, caused many states and localities to reevaluate their service delivery efforts and to explore new strategies for meeting the needs of children and families in a time of increasingly limited resources. Strategies included replacing lost federal support by using own-source revenues or other federal funds, setting service priorities, shifting responsibility to the local level or to the private sector, altering distribution formulas, and taking other direct cost-cutting actions.

Social Services

The social services block grant has been the dominant force in social services, followed by the community services block grant. In their use of the social services block-grant funds the states have generally given high priority to children's services, especially crisis-oriented services, and have been able to replace a significant amount of lost federal funding from social services block grants. Replacement funds have come from a variety of specific sources: from the state general funds, from shifting social service block grant funds away from other social services, or from intertitle transfer. This last source has involved primarily shifting day care costs to Title IV(A) through the child care "disregard" provision in AFDC (whereby child care expenses are deducted from income before an AFDC award is calculated) and shifting homemaker services costs to Title XIX through medicaid. Most types of social services have been maintained relatively well despite the severe federal losses; the major exception is day care services, which have lost ground significantly in many states. Local service providers have frequently turned to fee-for-service to sustain their programs. The group most affected by these changes is the working poor.

The reductions in community services block grants have been made differently from and with far less success than the reductions in social services grants. Numerous states have made formula changes to improve statewide service coverage, and many have bought local jurisdictions into the allocation process. In general, states and localities have not been successful in offsetting the revenue losses due to federal cutbacks.

Health Services

Creation of the three health block grants, coupled with changes in the medicaid program, led to substantial losses in federal funding for state and local health services for children. In terms of generating funds to replace the lost federal ones, the program providing maternal and child health services fared the least well of the three block grants; nonetheless, the majority of the states studied here increased total revenues for these services, both through added state funding and through use of carryover federal funds. The states expressed strong service priorities in all the health block grants. Most favored were broad-constituency programs that had previously been partially funded at the state and local level—for example, crippled children's services (maternal and child health program) and the hypertension program (preventive services program). Although jurisdiction showed no clear preference for or against children's services compared to services for other age groups, some programs particularly focusing on children suffered huge losses—for example, lead-based paint poisoning, sudden infant death syndrome, and rat control.

The greatest impact on children's health services came from changes in the medicaid program. The limitations on service coverage, added requirements for copayments, and tightening of medicaid eligibility that accompanied AFDC eligibility changes made health care more costly and less accessible to many poor families. The consequence of these health policy changes was that a wide range of problems were passed on to the local level and then to private providers and to families themselves through restrictions on service availability at local health clinics and the institution of fees for services.

Employment, Education and Income Support

Federal cuts were large in these program areas, and there was generally little supplementation with state or local funds. Youth employment monies decreased as a result of federal actions. Few jurisdictions reportedly sought to reverse that trend. States had very limited discretionary monies to spend on education and generally spent what little they had on general education improvements or on mandated services; suffering the most were compensatory education programs for the disadvantaged. States were quick to implement the AFDC changes regarding income maintenance, often because substantial cost savings could be obtained. Many states saved additional revenues by not raising payment standards. Some states increased general assistance payments because that program became the source of support for people eliminated from AFDC, but other states reduced general assistance grants in a broad effort to reduce costs in programs that were not federally supported. The AFDC changes had the greatest impact of all program changes, both in terms of the direct benefits and the eligibility linkage between AFDC and other social and health programs.

In all areas of state and local involvement, children's services have suffered reductions despite varying levels of public effort to remedy the federal changes. States and localities were able to replace some of the lost federal funds or to shift funds among different services in the block grant and categorical grant programs, but were largely unable to mediate the effects of changes in the large entitlement programs.

The Response of the Nonprofit Sector

The systematic reductions in a broad range of programs affecting children has pushed the problems beyond the resources of state and local governments to remedy. The Reagan administration has argued strongly that it is the private sector that can and will come to the aid of human services agencies and their recipients. Such a proposition, however, is difficult to implement. Nonprofit agencies are affected by government funding reductions in two ways: persons who lose support from government programs turn to nonprofit agencies for help, thus increasing the demand for services that the nonproft agencies provide; and the nonprofit agencies themselves lose government funding through cutbacks in service contracts. In fiscal 1982, 42 percent of the revenues of agencies serving children came from government (including federal, state, and local sources), a decrease of 3.4 percent in inflation-adjusted terms since fiscal 1981. This loss meant that the average nonprofit children's agency could not continue to serve the needy as it had in 1981 and earlier.

Not surprisingly, certain types of agencies serving children fared much worse than others. The hardest hit by government funding cuts were agencies primarily offering day care, other social services, education and research services (excluding schools), recreation activities, and employment and training services. Child health and mental health agencies and institutional and residential care facilities actually received increased government support.

In the face of substantial losses in government support for most service areas, nonprofit children's agencies sought alternative funding. Overall, they were able to more than replace the government cuts, registering a 2.1 percent increase in total expenditures between fiscal years 1981 and 1982, after adjusting for inflation. However, again the benefits were differentially spread among the agency types. Recreation agencies made the most dramatic recovery, due largely to their major reliance on service fees. Employment and training agencies, day care centers, and education and research organizations also did well, replacing most or all of their government losses. New revenues came largely from corporations and, in the case of day care, from United Way; and all increased their reliance on fees and charges for service. Social service agencies had the hardest time finding monies to replace their government losses, especially when faced with added losses in United Way support.

While many nonprofit agencies serving children were able to recover from government funding reductions, this was achieved largely by increasing their service fees and charges. Thus these agencies, because they have begun to rely heavily on service charges, have become less able to pick up the nonpaying persons who have lost public benefits and who most need help.

Outcomes for Children and Families

How have children and families coped with the program reductions, eligibility restrictions, and changes in service quality that resulted from the combined actions of federal, state, and local decision-makers? Three major patterns of behavior commonly have been observed. First, because fewer services were available at a price recipients could afford (that is, subsidized), recipients have tended to defer routine care or settled for lower quality care. Second, because many persons lost in-kind benefits and support services, they have turned more frequently to last-resort programs, such as the supplementary food program for women, infants, and children (WIC), general assistance, or hospital outpatient departments. Third, because they have deferred routine care and utilized services less suited to their needs, such recipients increasingly have faced crises in which outside help is immediately needed.

Many observers believe such behavioral patterns point to the need for a nationwide effort to address the problems facing children's services. Action has already begun at the federal level, in the activity of the House Select Committee on Children, Youth, and Families and in congressional action to restore some of the cuts to social programs. At the local level, public and nonprofit task forces and coalitions have been formed to deal with critical problems such as hunger, inadequate housing, and child abuse. By working together in developing service priorities, government and the nonprofit sector can explore ways to make more efficient use of their limited resources, with the goal of together providing the social services necessary to care for America's children.

CHAPTER 2

THE NATIONAL PICTURE

Widespread public concern for the health and general welfare needs of children in the United States has led to the creation of the House Select Committee on Children, Youth, and Families. In its first report the committee outlined the recent trends and current status of children in the United States. Table 1, which draws selected statistics from the report, shows the deteriorating economic circumstances of many households with children, particularly minority households and those with female heads of household.

In 1982, 19 percent of all families had female heads of household and one in five children lived with the mother only, compared to roughly half these proportions in 1970. Among black families the statistics present an even starker picture: 30 percent of families in 1970 and 46 percent in 1982 had female heads of household. Families with the mother as the sole source of support have particular difficulty making ends meet financially; in 1981 the median income of children in mother-only families was $8,653, which was 34 percent of that earned by husband-wife families in 1981 and which in real terms was 11 percent less than their median income in 1970. In 1982 more than 20 percent of all children lived in poverty, with black children about three times more likely than whites to be poor. In an effort to alleviate income problems the majority of mothers now work: in 1982 half of those with children under age six and two-thirds of other mothers were in the labor force.

The picture is not as bleak as the financial situation of these households seems to indicate. The health of children in general appears to be improving. Infant mortality in 1982 was 11 deaths per 1,000 live births, a decline from 20 deaths per 1,000 live births in 1970, although the rate for blacks remains nearly twice that for whites. More mothers, especially young ones, are entering prenatal care early with resulting improvements in the birth weight of their babies, and more infants are receiving timely immunizations. A serious problem still exists among

TABLE 1

SELECTED STATISTICS ON CHILDREN AND THEIR FAMILIES, 1970, 1980, AND 1982
(Percent unless otherwise indicated)

Measure	1970	1980	1982
Number of children under age 18 (millions)	70	64	63
Children living below poverty level[a]	15	18	21
White	11	13	17
Black	42	42	47
Families with female heads	10	17	19
White	8	13	5
Black	30	47	46
Children living with mother only	11	n.a.	20
Mothers in labor force with children under age 5	32	n.a.	50
Mothers in labor force with children ages 6 through 17	52	n.a.	66
Infant mortality (deaths per 1,000 live births)	20	13	11
Ratio of live births in which prenatal care began in first trimester to no prenatal care			
All mothers	68/0	76/1	74/1
Mothers under age 15	n.a.	34/5	40/6
Mothers ages 15 to 19	n.a.	56/3	53/3

SOURCES: U.S. Congress, House Select Committee on Children, Youth, and Families,
   U.S. Children and Their Families: Current Conditions and Recent Trends,
   98th Cong., 1st sess. (Washington, D.C.: U.S. Government Printing Office,
   May 1983).
   n.a. Not available.
   a. The poverty level is based on money income and does not reflect receipt of noncash

teenage mothers, who are much less likely than older women to receive prenatal care early or indeed at all.

These figures point to the pressing needs of children and their families for supportive services of many kinds, especially three major federally supported programs: aid to families with dependent children (AFDC), medicaid, and food stamps. The proportion of families receiving these benefits grew modestly between 1970 and 1980, but the trend did not continue. Indeed, the percentage of children on AFDC fell between 1980 and 1981, even though the median income of families with children dropped and the proportion of children living in poverty rose during that time. The general implication is clearly that life has become much more difficult for families with children and that public services have not adequately alleviated the economic and social hardships. The remainder of this chapter examines the reductions in

TABLE 1 (*Continued*)

Measure	1970	1980	1982
Infants with low birth weight			
All mothers	8	7	7
Mothers with no prenatal care	n.a.	22	n.a.
Immunized children ages 1 to 4			
Measles	57	64	64[c]
Rubella	37	64	65[c]
DPT[b]	76	66	68[c]
Polio	66	59	60[c]
Median family income of families children			
living in families (constant 1981 dollars)[d]			
All families	23,954	23,111	22,041[c]
Husband-wife family	25,860	26,319	25,636[c]
Mother-only family	9,708	8,761	8,653[c]
Children receiving AFDC	9	12	11[c]
Recipient families with children			
School lunches	15[c]	16	16[c]
Food stamps	12[e]	13	14[c]
Medicaid	12[e]	13	13[c]

benefits. Different levels are set according to the size and composition of the family. The levels are revised each year according to the consumer price index. In 1982, for example, the average annual income for a family of four living at the poverty level was $9,862.

b. Diptheria, pertussis, and tetanus.

c. Data are for 1981.

d. Medians are based on children; that is, each child is characterized by the income of its family, and the median for all children is computed.

e. Data are for 1979.

federal expenditures that have led to the inadequacy of children's services; subsequent chapters look at the effects of these actions on state and local agencies providing services for children and on nonprofit agencies providing similar services.

Federal Programs for Children

A number of federal government agencies have programs that affect the lives of children, both directly by the services they offer to children or their families and indirectly by improving the environment in which they live. In 1979, declared the international year for the child, a federal interagency committee formed to work for children prepared a document briefly describing some of the myriad of federal efforts that affect the lives of children.[1] Included were more than twenty-five federal agencies in the United States that sponsor over 250 children's service programs. In this examination of the effects of the Reagan administration on the health and general welfare of children, I concentrate on only those federal programs that have the most direct impact on children (24 programs; see table 2). These twenty-four federal programs form the nucleus of the federal government's mandate to serve children in the broad areas of social service, health, nutrition, education, employment, and income assistance.

Social Services

The keystone of social service programs for children is the social services block grant program, which was transformed by the Omnibus Budget Reconciliation Act of 1981 (hereafter reconciliation act) from the Title XX program. Enacted in 1974, Title XX was in its own right a quasi-block grant because it allowed states considerable flexibility in setting service priorities and funding levels. Child-related services included day care, counseling, information and referral, legal services, protective services, foster care, homemaker assistance and other in-home services. The shift to a formal block grant brought several important changes: elimination of required state matching funds; merging of previously separate federal appropriations for the social services, staff training, and child care provided by Title XX; and removal of the mandate to expend 50 percent of funds on welfare recipients. In addition, in the area of child care, the Department of Health and Human Services had recently published the federal inter-agency day care requirements after a laborious development phase. The reconciliation act rendered these regulations moot, despite substantial efforts already made by states and local service providers to adjust their practices to the impending federal requirements.

On average the states spend about half their funds from social services block grants on child welfare services. The funds decreased 15 percent in real terms between fiscal years 1981 and 1982 and fell an additional 5 percent in fiscal 1983 (table 3). In fiscal 1984 the funds showed a rise of nearly 7 percent due to the increased monies contained in the appropriations bill for the departments of labor and of health and human services, which was passed by Congress for the first time in five years. Nonetheless, the three-year period yielded a net loss of over 13 percent in inflation-adjusted terms.

1. U.S. Department of Health, Education, and Welfare, *Report on Federal Government Programs that Relate to Children* (Washington, D.C.: U.S. Government Printing Office, 1979).

TABLE 2

FEDERAL PROGRAMS DIRECTLY AFFECTING CHILDREN, FISCAL 1983

Federal Programs	Administering Agency	Legislative Authority
Social services		
Social services block grant (Title XX)	Department of Health and Human Services (DHHS), Office of Human Development Services	Social Security Act (SSA), Title XX[a]
Child welfare services	DHHS, Children's Bureau	SSA, Title IV(B)
Foster care and adoption assistance	DHHS, Children's Bureau (previously DHHS, Social Security Administration)	SSA, Title IV(E), previously IV(A)
Child abuse and neglect	DHHS, Children's Bureau	Child Abuse Prevention and Treatment Act of 1974
Work incentive program child care	DHHS, Office of Human Development Services	SSA, Title IV(C)
Head Start	DHHS, Office of Developmental Services	Economic Opportunity and Community Partnership Act of 1974, Title V
Juvenile justice and delinquency prevention	Department of Justice, Office of Juvenile Justice and Delinquency Prevention	Juvenile Justice and Delinquency Prevention Act of 1974
Runaway youth	DHHS, Youth Development Bureau	Juvenile Justice and Delinquency Prevention Act, Title III
Community services	DHHS, Office of Community Affairs (previously Community Services Administration)	Economic Opportunity Act of 1964[a]
Health		
Maternal and child health	DHHS, Health Services Administration (HSA)	SSA, Title V, Public Health Service Act[a]
Preventive health	DHHS, HSA	Public Health Service Act, Health Services and Centers Amendments of 1978[a]

TABLE 2 (*Continued*)

Federal Programs	Administering Agency	Legislative Authority
Medicaid	DHHS, Health Care Financing Administration	SSA, Title XIX
Mental health	DHHS, Alcohol, Drug Abuse, and Mental Health Administration	Community Mental Health Centers Act[a]
Adolescent family life	DHHS, Office of Population Affairs	Public Health Service Act, Title XX
Nutrition		
Supplemental food program for women, infants, and children	DHHS (previously Food and Nutrition Service, Department of Agriculture)	Child Nutrition Act of 1966
School breakfast and lunch programs	Food and Nutrition Service, Department of Agriculture	National School Lunch Act
Child care and summer feeding programs	Department of Agriculture	Child Nutrition Act of 1966
Food stamps	Department of Agriculture	Food Stamp Act of 1977
Education		
Compensatory education	Department of Education	ESEA of 1965, Title I and Education Consolidation and Improvement Act of 1981, Chapter 1
Education for handicapped	Department of Education	Education for All Handicapped Act of 1975
Employment		
Youth training	Department of Labor Employment and Training Administration, Office of Youth Programs	Comprehensive Employment and Training Act, Title III
Income assistance		
AFDC	DHHS, Social Security Administration	SSA, Title IV(A)

SOURCE: Public documents related to federal legislations for 1983.
  a. Redesigned under the Omnibus Budget Reconciliation Act to form block grants.

in five years. Nonetheless, the three-year period yielded a net loss of over 13 years in inflation-adjusted terms.

The social service programs most clearly directed to children are Titles IV(B) and IV(E), generally designated as child welfare services. These services include foster care, adoption, protective services, preventive-supportive services to children in their own homes, and day care unrelated to employment. Funding for most of these services comes through Title IV(B); Title IV(E) provides foster care and adoption assistance. Created in the Adoption Assistance and Child Welfare Act of 1980, Title IV(E) replaces Title IV(A) foster care, which provided limited federal reimbursement for foster care for AFDC-eligible children, conditional on federal appropriations for Title IV(B): if and only if Title IV(B) funding reaches a certain level, Title IV(E) foster care funds will be constrained. Only in 1981 have appropriations reached the necessary level to trigger the cap on foster care. Title IV(E) additionally makes available for the first time federal adoption assistance payments to facilitate the permanent placement of children with special needs.[2] Although the Adoption Assistance and Child Welfare Act of 1980 was enacted under the Carter administration and was not directly affected by the reconciliation act, the Reagan administration proposed in 1983 a consolidation into a child welfare services block grant, an action which, if it had passed, would have eliminated the role of the federal government that was central to the previous legislation.

Like the social services block grant, Titles IV(B) and IV(E) faced large percentage losses between fiscal years 1981 and 1982, which seriously hampered states' implementation of the prevention and reunification thrust of the 1980 act. Underscoring this point, Title IV(E) foster care expenditures increased dramatically in fiscal years 1983 and 1984, leaving the program well ahead of inflation for the three-year period. This growth suggests that without increased funds for Title IV(B) the federal government could not constrain Title IV(E) costs, nor could states shift children from foster care to home-based care. Indeed, Title IV(B) outlays continued to decrease in fiscal 1983. Despite fiscal 1984 estimates that show child welfare services keeping pace with inflation, Title IV(B) weathered substantial losses between 1981 and 1984.

A small federal program closely related to Title IV(B) child welfare services is child abuse and neglect prevention. The state-grants portion

---

2. In general these children are defined as handicapped, minority, older, or members of a sibling group.

TABLE 3

FEDERAL OUTLAYS FOR PROGRAMS AFFECTING CHILDREN, SELECTED FISCAL YEARS 1981–84

Program	Outlays in 1981 ($ millions)	Percent Real Change			
		1981–82	1982–83	1983–84	1981–84
Social services and child care					
Social services block grant, Title XX	2,813	−14.9	−4.8	6.7	−13.5
Child welfare, Title IV(B)[a]	178	−15.2	−3.0	1.2	−16.7
Foster care and adoption assistance,[a] Title IV(E) programs[a]	328	−8.0	21.3	6.6	19.0
Child abuse and neglect	7	−5.6	−3.0	−4.2	−12.3
Head Start	766	2.6	2.7	4.1	9.7
Work incentive program child care[b]	115	−23.7	88.9	−100.0	−100.0
Juvenile justice and delinquency prevention and runaway youth programs[a]	117	−36.3	−3.0	30.0	−19.8
Community services block grant	619	−61.4	33.9	0.8	−48.0
Total social services	4,943	−18.3	3.1	1.7	−14.4
Health					
Medicaid	16,948	−2.9	5.6	2.1	4.8
Maternal and child health block grant	398	22.3	−19.7	−4.2	−5.9
Preventive health and health services block grant	118	0.7	−8.4	−30.0	−35.3
Mental health[a]	659	−23.3	−1.0	−2.3	−25.7
Adolescent family life	4	88.7	33.4	13.2	185.1
Total health	18,127	−3.0	4.6	1.7	3.2

Nutrition					
Food stamps	11,253	−7.7	4.3	−11.6	−14.8
School breakfast and school lunch programs[a]	1,088	−35.7	4.2	−11.5	−40.7
Child care and summer food programs[a]	444	−23.5	15.1	−25.7	−34.6
				.	
Women, infants, and children supplementary food programs	930	−5.6	16.7[b]	−7.7[b]	1.6
Total nutrition	13,715	−10.3	5.5	−11.7	−16.4
Other					
Compensatory education	3,354	−16.9	−13.1	22.2	−11.7
Education for handicapped	1,035	4.0	9.7	−17.7	6.1
CETA youth training[c]	2,369	−50.3	4.9	−10.1	−53.1
AFDC	8,176	−7.8	−4.4	−8.5	−19.3
Total	51,719	−10.1	2.3	−3.3	−11.0

SOURCES: Unpublished federal outlay analysis tables for fiscal 1980–82; appendixes of *Budget of the United States Government* for fiscal years 1983 and 1984.

a. Obligations; outlays not available.
b. Estimated outlays for the work incentive program.
c. As mandated by the Comprehensive Employment and Training Act of 1973.

of the program supports state agencies that respond to reports of abuse and neglect, while the demonstration portion funds special projects in child abuse and neglect prevention and treatment. In fiscal 1982 the Reagan administration sought unsuccessfully to eliminate the program. Its outlays have remained at a steady level in current dollars, but with losses each year due to inflation.

Child care programs are a major part of children's social services. In fiscal 1982 approximately 20 percent of all funds from social services block grants were spent on day care. The major reductions in these block grant funds have thus directly affected child care programs; Children's Defense Fund reports that 1983 expenditures on day care were 14 percent below the 1981 Title XX level even before adjusting for inflation.[3] Other sources of funding for child care include the AFDC "income disregard,"[4] the child care tax credit,[5] and child care as mandated by the work incentive program. This program provides care for the children of low-income parents participating in work or training programs. It suffered a substantial cutback in fiscal 1982, temporarily recovered in fiscal 1983, and is slated for elimination in 1984.

Head Start is a special form of child day care established to offer early childhood development programs for economically disadvantaged preschool children. In fiscal 1982 enrollment was 396,000 children.[6] It is one of few federal children's programs that has consistently been well supported. Head Start grew at a steady rate of 3 to 4 percent each year between 1981 and 1984, thus registering a healthy growth rate of nearly 10 percent beyond inflation for the three-year period. It is the only children's social service that witnessed increased federal funding in fiscal 1982.

The only federal social services programs clearly aimed at the justice system are the juvenile justice and delinquency prevention programs and the runaway youth programs. Both created under the Juvenile Justice and Delinquency Prevention Act of 1974, these programs are designed to deter juvenile crime and delinquency, and

---

3. Helen Blank, *Children and Federal Child Care Cuts: A National Survey of the Impact of Federal Title XX Cuts on State Child Care Systems* (Washington, D.C.: Children's Defense Fund, 1983), p. 5.

4. The AFDC provision allows recipients to deduct from their income $160 a month for child care expenses for each child before benefits are calculated.

5. The Economic Recovery Tax Act of 1981 raised the maximum credit that can be taken and expanded the credit to families in lower income brackets. However, low-income families who do not pay taxes cannot benefit from this deduction.

6. House Select Committee on Children, Youth, and Families, *U.S. Children and Their Families: Current Conditions and Recent Trends,* 98 Cong., 1st sess. (Washington, D.C.: U.S. Government Printing Office, May 1983).

to remove juveniles from adult jails and nonoffenders and status offenders from detention facilities. States receive formula grants to improve their juvenile justice systems; special grants are also available for prevention programs. The Reagan administration has sought in each of its budgets to eliminate these programs, declaring that "the principal objectives of the program have been achieved to the extent which is practicable."[7] Federal funding decreased 36 percent between fiscal years 1981 and 1982, after adjusting for inflation, and an additional 3 percent by fiscal 1983. In fiscal 1984, however, Congress passed the State Justice Bill, which increased funding from the previous fiscal year by 30 percent and thus replaced a portion of the losses from the previous two years.

The last program included in table 3 under social services is the community services block grant. In 1981 the reconciliation act abolished the Community Services Administration, an independent agency, and transferred responsibility to the Office of Community Affairs in the Department of Health and Human Services. The block grant provides funds for community-based programs in health, nutrition, housing, and employment services for low-income families. These services primarily (but not exclusively) benefit poor families having children. The shift to the block grant removed the states' matching requirement and increased state flexibility regarding service priorities and target populations but maintained a strong earmarking requirement for funding of agencies involved in the community action program. The program suffered real losses of 61 percent in fiscal 1982, significantly more than any other social services program affecting children. Gains occurred in fiscal years 1983 and 1984, but funding remained far below the Community Services Administration level.

As a whole, social service programs affecting children fared worse than the other broad groups of programs listed in table 3; a loss of 18 percent in inflation-adjusted dollars occurred between 1981 and 1982; modest increases in outlays the following two years raised this loss to 14 percent for the three-year period. The reconciliation act directly affected only two of the eight social services programs listed in the table—the social services block grant and the community services block grant. However, because these block grants are two of the three largest sources of funds for children's social services and together account for 60 to 70 percent of the federal social services outlays,

---

7. *Budget of the United States Government, FY 1984 Appendix* (Washington, D.C.: U.S. Government Printing Office, 1983), p. I–N23.

aggregate social services spending clearly reflects the block grant funding levels.

Although social services programs account for less than one-tenth of the federal outlays to children listed in the table, they constitute the major component of the network of children's services. More than programs in other service areas, many social services programs are specifically directed toward children's needs; thus changes in federal spending in these programs may have particularly noticeable effects on children. It is for this reason that the focus here is primarily on social services, with less attention to health services, nutrition services, and income-support programs that complement social services assistance.

Health Services

Five health programs constitute the majority of federally supported health services for children. The largest of these is the medicaid program, which provides routine and special medical care for poor families. Children constituted 48 percent of all medicaid recipients in 1982, and 13 percent of all payments went for children's care.[8] Included in medicaid is a special children's health program, the early periodic screening, diagnosis and testing program. The Reagan administration twice unsuccessfully proposed repeal of some or all of this program.

Medicaid outlays showed a modest decrease of 3 percent from fiscal years 1981 to 1982, largely through reconciliation act changes that reduced federal cost-sharing and increased state discretion over eligibility and reimbursement levels. The reconciliation act also increased copayments for many poor people (eligible children and pregnant women were exempted) and made numerous changes in the list of reimbursable expenses under medicaid. The use of health care by poor families was thus affected, both because of the families' limited ability to meet the copayment requirement and because of the more limited availability (as providers found it financially necessary to serve a greater proportion of non-medicaid patients).[9] In fiscal years 1983 and 1984 medicaid outlays rose modestly; this was due largely to the increased demand for medicaid-subsidized health care that arose from the declining federal funding for the health block-grant programs.

---

8. House Select Committee on Children, Youth, and Families, *U.S. Children and Their Families,* p. 53.

9. Randall R. Bovbjerg and John Holahan, *Medicaid in the Reagan Era: Federal Policy and State Choices* (Washington, D.C.: Urban Institute Press, 1982).

Outlays for fiscal 1984 are estimated to be more than $20 billion, which makes medicaid growth nearly 5 percent for the 1981–84 period.

The health program most clearly aimed at children's health needs is the maternal and child health block grant. Created under the reconciliation act, the block grant consolidated eight separate programs: Title V maternal and child health services, crippled children's services, and services related to lead-based paint poisoning, adolescent pregnancy, genetics testing, sudden infant death syndrome, hemophilia, and disabled children (supplemental social security income program). States were allowed much greater flexibility than in the past regarding maternal and child health service priorities, funding levels, and providers, because service requirements and reporting requirements were eliminated and because all grants began to flow through the states rather than from the federal agency directly to local grantees.

The block grant program for maternal and child health began auspiciously in the Reagan years with 22 percent growth between fiscal years 1981 and 1982. This appears to have been a one-year event, however, as fiscal 1983 outlays fell 20 percent and fiscal 1984 shows an estimated 4 percent real loss from the already lower level of fiscal 1983, leaving spending below the fiscal 1981 level (after adjusting for inflation). Maternal and infant care remains a high priority in most states; the cuts more often have affected the other services such as programs to prevent lead-based paint poisoning, genetics and hemophilia demonstration projects, and disabled children's programs (supplemental security income).[10]

Two other health programs that address the needs of children are the preventive health and health services block grant and the alcohol, drug abuse, and mental health block grant. Preventive health consolidates seven formerly distinct service programs and one new program: health education and risk reduction, focusing on smoking and substance abuse in secondry schools, hypertension, fluoridation, urban rat control, emergency medical services, health incentive grants for comprehensive public health services, home health services, and a newly funded program called rape prevention services. The largest of these, comprehensive health services, has the most direct effect on children because it was commonly used to support local health department services that included childhood immunizations.[11] The block grant

10. Eugene C. Durman, Barbara A. Davis, and Randall R. Bovbjerg, "Block Grants and the New Federalism: The Second Year Experience," Contract Report (Washington, D.C.: Urban Institute, April 1984).

11. Immunizations are also given at community health centers under the primary care block grant. This grant did not take effect until fiscal 1983.

offered states an opportunity to reallocate funds to programs higher in the state's priorities, although there were congressional mandates regarding funding levels for several of the preceding programs. The preventive health and health services block grant kept pace with inflation in fiscal 1982 but lost much ground in fiscal years 1983 and 1984.

The alcohol, drug abuse, and mental health block grant combines numerous service programs that previously received separate funding. Only the third area, mental health, affects children in any significant way through services offered by community mental health centers. The creation of the block grant had important implications for children's mental health services: no such services were earmarked in the block grant, despite congressional passage in 1981 of the Mental Health Systems Act (soon repealed by the reconciliation act), which provided states and localities with funds to improve services for seriously disturbed children and adolescents. Mental health services available through the block grant decreased by 23 percent in fiscal 1982 and continued to lose minimally to inflation in subsequent years. The result was an aggregate loss of over 25 percent for the three-year period. In 1983, however, mental health services for children received a boost with the passage of a new children's mental health initiative, funded at $1.5 million.

The adolescent family life program, funded under Title XX of the Public Health Services Act, provides a broad range of services to adolescents who are pregnant, who are parents, or who are at high risk of teenage parenthood. Included are social services, education and employment services, and health services, although prenatal care and pediatric care are the core services in many of the local projects. Grants are awarded on a competitive basis to public or nonprofit organizations. Funding has increased steadily since the program was enacted in 1981. The program nevertheless remains a minor part of overall expenditures on children's health services.

Nutrition

Six nutrition programs benefit children and their families. Although the largest of these, the food stamps program, is not exclusively for children, over half of the 22 million people participating in the food stamps program in 1982 were children.[12] Food stamp outlays declined

---

12. House Select Committee on Children, Youth, and Families, *U.S. Children and Their Families;* and Children's Defense Fund, *A Children's Defense Budget: An Analysis of the President's Budget and Children* (Washington, D.C.: CDF, 1984).

by nearly 8 percent in fiscal 1982, due to reconciliation act changes that lowered basic benefit levels, reduced the income deduction for working families, lowered the income limits, and decreased benefits for many renters. Outlays bounced back in fiscal 1983, as the food stamp rolls expanded with increasing numbers of poor and unemployed. Expenditures for fiscal 1984 were estimated to be down substantially from the high of fiscal 1983, however, leaving the program nearly 15 percent behind inflation by fiscal 1984.

For many families the losses in food stamp benefits make school-based food programs even more important in guaranteeing that children are provided with good nutrition. The school lunch program is the oldest of the child nutrition programs. For some or no payment, school lunches went to an average of 23.6 million children each school day in 1982. School breakfast programs are less highly utilized but are equally important for the nutritional needs of low-income children. The reconciliation act lowered eligibility limits for free and reduced-price meals and reduced subsidies for lunches, causing many schools to withdraw from the program. Funding fell 36 percent in 1982 and fell again by 12 percent in 1984. This has occurred largely because of the Reagan administration's contention that too many nonpoor children were benefiting. In fact, most of the funds purchase meals for low-income children: about 80 percent of the funds for the school lunch and more than 95 percent of the funds for the school breakfast programs.[13]

The preschool equivalent of the school breakfast and lunch programs is the child care food program; the equivalent for meals after the school year ends is the summer food service program. The majority of these meals go to poor children. Cuts resulting from the reconciliation act have reduced the number of meals that can be served in day care centers and homes that provide family day care and have eliminated the many summer food programs that are not operated by school systems or local governments. Funding decreased by one-quarter in fiscal 1982, and even more sharply again in fiscal 1984. The reduction in federal reimbursement for these and the school-based meals, and the restrictions on eligible providers of child care, have both increased the cost to the institutions that continue to participate and greatly reduced the availability of the subsidized meals.

The WIC program, a special supplemental food program for women, infants, and children, is an important and highly successful nutrition program; it is the nutrition program of last resort. Usually

13. Children's Defense Fund, *A Children's Defense Budget*, p. 118.

run through local health clinics, it offers food supplements (such as infant formula, milk, and eggs) and nutrition counseling to low-income pregnant and nursing women, infants, and young children. In 1982 this program served 2.4 million people. Funding failed to keep pace with inflation in fiscal 1982 and again in fiscal 1984; in fiscal 1983 it grew by 17 percent, as increasing numbers of persons were determined by health professionals to be at nutritional risk. For the three-year period the program just managed to keep pace with inflation, with a 1.6 percent growth rate.

Education, Employment and Income Assistance

The four remaining programs listed in table 3 are among the largest of the federal programs affecting children and have the longest-term results. Compensatory education for disadvantaged (ESEA, Title I) includes instruction in reading and mathematics for educationally disadvantaged children living in low-income areas, and the Education for the Handicapped Act (P.L. 94-142) makes schools and special education services available to all handicapped children. The reconciliation act replaced ESEA, Title I with Chapter 1 of the Education Consolidation and Improvement Act, which lessened the focus on children most in need and increased state discretion. Compensatory education lost 17 percent of its federal support in fiscal 1982 and more in fiscal 1983; increased funds in fiscal 1984 reduced the loss to 12 percent. The education for the handicapped program has fared much better, experiencing real growth between fiscal years 1981 and 1984 even though it suffered a large percentage decrease in fiscal 1984. The program expansion has occurred despite repeated administration efforts to fold the program into an education block grant.

Children are also affected both directly through youth employment programs and indirectly through employment and training programs designed for their parents. The Comprehensive Employment and Training Act of 1973 as a whole was eliminated by the Reagan administration, replaced by the Job Training Partnership Act. Youth training lost half its funding, $1.1 billion, between fiscal years 1981 and 1982; the three-year period showed a net loss of even more.

The fate of poor childen perhaps hangs most heavily on the intricacies of the aid to families with dependent children program, which provides much-needed income. Participation in this program is the criterion for categorical eligibility in many other federal programs. Nearly all AFDC assistance goes to households with female heads. More than 7.0 million children in 3.6 million families received AFDC benefits in 1981; these children represent over 11 percent of all children under eighteen years of age.[14]

The AFDC program is an appropriated entitlement, meaning that appropriations are necessary but cannot be used to control AFDC expenditures. The reconciliation act sought to control AFDC spending by reducing federal requirements and by limiting state discretion. The most significant changes included reduced income disregards, stricter calculation of income for eligibility determination, restrictions on categorical eligibility, and work requirements in exchange for benefits. The change that most directly affected children was the elimination of payments for children over age eighteen and for pregnant women before the sixth month of pregnancy. As a result of all these changes, AFDC outlays have decreased each year since the reconciliation act was passed, accumulating to a 19 percent loss between fiscal years 1981 and 1984. The number of participating families and children has similarly decreased by an estimated 400,000 to 500,000.[15]

Total outlays for the twenty-five federal programs affecting children decreased most sharply between fiscal years 1981 and 1982, largely as a result of policy changes contained in the reconciliation act. The real loss of 10 percent registered in fiscal 1982 stemmed primarily from cutbacks in the food stamps program (a decrease of $900 million in 1981 prices) and in youth training (a decrease of $1 billion in 1981 prices). Twenty of the twenty-five children's services programs failed to keep pace with inflation between 1981 and 1982, and the majority suffered sizable losses even in nominal terms. Fiscal 1983 saw a modest increase beyond inflation, almost exclusively due to increased outlays under medicaid. The outlays for fiscal 1984 are again estimated to be reduced by 3 perecent, leaving total outlays 11 percent below the fiscal 1981 level in inflation-adjusted terms.

Significance of Reductions for State and Local Government Budgets

It is difficult to specify the precise budgetary effect of federal cutbacks on state and local governments as a whole, especially for programs as diverse as those considered here. One can gain a sense

14. House Select Committee on Children, Youth, and Families, *U.S. Children and Their Families*.

15. John L. Palmer and Isabel V. Sawhill, eds., *The Reagan Record* (Cambridge, Mass.: Ballinger, 1984).

TABLE 4

FEDERAL GOVERNMENT'S SHARE OF SPENDING IN SIXTEEN LOCAL COMMUNITIES,
FISCAL 1982

| | Percentage of Site Funding From Federal Government | | |
Program Area	Median Site[a]	Site with High Percentage	Site with Low Percentage
Health	71	92	40
Social services	58	91	33
Employment and training	99	100	87
Income assistance	75	96	56

SOURCE: Nonprofit sector project. See Stephen Rozman and James C. Musselwhite, Jr., *Government Spending and the Nonprofit Sector in Two Mississippi Communities: Jackson/Hinds County and Vicksburg/Warren County* (Washington, D.C.: Urban Institute Press, 1985), Table 2.7, p. 30.

a. For the sixteen communities the median site was the midpoint between the sites ranked eighth and ninth in terms of percentage of federal funding.

of the impact, however, by examining in several communities the share of public spending that comes from the federal government for particular services. The Urban Institute has recently conducted an analysis of twelve metropolitan areas and four rural counties to determine public spending patterns for services in six program areas (health, social services, subsidized employment and training, income assistance, housing and community development, and arts and recreation).[16] The first four of these program areas have counterparts at the metropolitan level that are most congruent with the federal programs discussed in this chapter, although the data on spending do not separate revenues earmarked for children.

Table 4 indicates the extent of local community reliance on federal funds for services in the four program areas. Employment and training is clearly the service area most dependent on federal funding and thus most vulnerable to federal cutbacks. Health and income assistance are also heavily dependent on federal funds, but the variation among the sixteen sites (twelve metropolitan, four rural) suggests that some communities make notable efforts to use state and local monies to balance federal dependence. The program area showing the greatest variability is social services; here the low dependence of the median

16. An ongoing analysis of government spending conducted by the Nonprofit Sector project at The Urban Institute. Details are contained in the appendix.

site[17] on federal funding may be misleading because the range from the high site to the low site is so wide; it is clearly a program area that is hard to characterize with a single statistic.

Overall, it is clear that federal funds are pivotal in the delivery of public human services. The sensitivity of local governments to federal cutbacks varies greatly, but it is the rare locality that finds itself immune to federal policy changes, even in a single program area. The next chapter examines in detail the impact of federal retrenchment on state and local governments, focusing on ways in which public authorities have chosen to cope with lowered federal support and, often, increased service needs in their communities.

---

17. When the sites are ranked by percentage of program area funding coming from the federal government, the "high" site is the one with the highest percentage, the "low" site, the one with the lowest; and the "median" site is at the midpoint of the ranking—that is, as many sites have lower pecentages than the median site as have higher percentages.

CHAPTER 3

THE RESPONSE OF STATE AND LOCAL GOVERNMENT

The cutbacks in federal funding for children's programs have a varied impact on state and local governments. This chapter closely examines the effects of these cutbacks and the strategies that state and local governments use in responding, with a focus on the social services and health services programs.[1] The strategies include replacing lost federal support with own-source revenues or other federal funds, setting service priorities, shifting responsibility to the local level, altering distribution formulas, and taking other direct cost-cutting actions.

State and local responses to federal funding reductions varied substantially among the different children's service programs, depending on the funding structure of the federal program and the characteristics of the community. Three funding patterns are represented in the twenty-four children's programs discussed here: formula grants, in either block or categorical forms, available to all jurisdictions; entitlement programs given to all eligible recipients and having no absolute budget limits; and project grants awarded on a competitive basis to public or private agencies. Block and categorical grants are the most common form among children's programs. Reductions in funding for formula grant programs are generally pro rata, with each jurisdiction

---

1. This chapter is based on findings from three major studies conducted by The Urban Institute in 1982 and 1983. The first was a study, funded by the Department of Health and Human Services, of the effects of federal grant-in-aid programs on child welfare services in six states. The study analyzed both the fiscal and programmatic effects of the social services block grants and the Adoption Assistance and Child Welfare Act of 1980 (Public Law 96–272). A second, related study, also supported by the Department of Health and Human Services, examined the influence of federal block-grant action on state human services programs in eighteen states. The third study, which was funded by The Urban Institute's Changing Domestic Priorities project, explored the community-level effects of recent changes in federal domestic policy in four cities— Detroit, Boston, San Diego, and Richmond (Virginia). This chapter focuses on the findings of the two state-level studies, with the community-based study supplementing the discussion of state actions.

receiving the same proportionate reduction. Funding for the six block-grant programs—social services block grants; community services block grants; maternal and child health block grants; preventive services block grants; alcohol, drug abuse, and mental health block grants; and Chapter 2 of the Education Consolidation and Improvement Act—is distributed by formula determined in the enacting legislation, most of the programs utilizing the same state shares mandated under the previous categorical service-specific programs that were consolidated into the block grant. These categorical programs were also formula-based, with two exceptions: many of the programs consolidated into the preventive health and health services block grant were competitive project grants, as was Emergency School Aid Act (now part of the education block grant). In addition, six other children's programs are formula-based categorical programs: Title IV(B) child welfare services, Head Start, the supplemental food program for women, infants, and children (WIC), the work incentive program (WIN), one part of the juvenile justice and delinquency prevention program, and programs created by the Job Training Partnership Act.

Federal cutbacks similarly occurred in entitlement programs. Because of the open-ended nature of such programs, the federal government cannot directly control state spending through the appropriation process. It must change state program design by altering eligibility criteria or service coverage. The savings are always approximate because the modifications they make in rules cannot control exactly how many potential eligible recipients will become participants or how much those participants will use program services. The entitlement programs, the mainstays of the support system for the poor, are aid to families with dependent children (AFDC), medicaid, child nutrition programs (school breakfast and lunch programs, child care food programs, and summer food service programs), food stamps, compensatory education, and education for the handicapped.[2]

In many of the entitlement programs the states as well as the federal government can make changes in eligibility or payment levels. AFDC has perhaps the greatest state discretion, with states responsible for setting need levels and payment standards and also for choosing among numerous options in the federal legislation. Under the medicaid program the states are free to set their own reimbursement limits for

---

2. The last two programs providing education are closed-end entitlements—although all eligible persons are guaranteed assistance under these programs, Congress appropriates limited funds so the federal share varies by locality.

hospitals and physicians and to restrict service coverage in various ways. These and other issues are discussed in detail below.

In addition to formula grants and entitlements, federal funds also are available to states from special project grants, which are awarded on a competitive basis. A state may receive several or none of these grants, depending on the criteria used to select grantees. Often the grantee is not a state government office or even a local government agency, but rather a service organization in the private sector. Program funds are distributed as project grants in areas such as child abuse and neglect, juvenile justice and delinquency prevention, runaway youth, and adolescent family life. Before the creation of the block grants for health services, the categorical lead-based paint poisoning, rat control, and hypertension programs were also competitively funded.

Because project grants often bypass state and local governments and are generally much smaller than formula grants and entitlement programs, in general they are the most difficult to track on a state-by-state basis and have little direct effect on the service delivery of state and local governments. The following discussion, therefore, places most emphasis on entitlement programs and formula grant programs, including both block and categorical grants, especially in the areas of health and social services.

In the face of federal funding reduction of over 10 percent between fiscal years 1981 and 1982 in twenty-four programs affecting children, state and local governments took a number of actions to cope with the tighter budgetary situation. The federal cutbacks not coincidentally came at the same time as many states and localities were facing fiscal stresses of their own during the nationwide recession. State and local actions in the wake of passage of the Omnibus Budget Reconciliation Act of 1981 thus reflect the interaction of the fiscal health of the state and the local government, the extent of its federal revenue losses, and the importance of particular children's services relative to other state or local responsibilities. A jurisdiction with a strong commitment to children may nonetheless show decreasing support of children's services because of poor fiscal conditions; a jurisdiction that devotes increasing funds to children's services may in fact be moving from a very low level to a modest level of support for those services. The following analysis attempts to put in a broader context the changes in funding for children's services, by considering not only actual dollar amounts but also shifts in the relative shares of funds going to particular areas. In addition, attention is given to state and local choices regarding eligibility criteria, payment schedules, and other specific cost-cutting efforts because they provide an insight to implicit priorities given to service programs and beneficiaries.

Replacement of Lost Federal Funds

On a dollar-for-dollar basis, replacement of lost federal funds by states has been fairly extensive in the services included in the social services block grants and in the services included in three types of health block grants (maternal and child health grants, preventive health service grants, and alcohol, drug abuse, and mental health grants). It is important to note three important points, however. First, the dollar-for-dollar replacement does nothing to erase the effects of inflation; as is shown below, states only infrequently were able to produce as many "replacement dollars" as were lost and rarely compensated for inflation also.

Second, state replacement of block-grant monies seems to suggest a state commitment to a group of services as a whole, rather than to the discrete services that make up that block-grant group. In fact, states operate (and may continue to do so) on a more piecemeal basis by preferring to fund, for example, child protective services rather than information and referral, or crippled children's programs rather than programs to prevent lead-based paint poisoning. These intrablock choices are discussed in detail below in the section entitled "Priorities among Services"; the relevant point here is that what appears to be state support for a service genre may be an indication of a particularly strong preference for one service.

Third, as far as state general funds are concerned, replacement is basically a zero-sum game. If a state substantially increases its contribution to one service program, it probably decreases its support to several other programs. Replacement must be seen for what it is and nothing more: a reflection of a state's specific service priorities in the context of inflation and competing demands.

Social Services

Replacement of lost social services funds was common among the eighteen states surveyed in 1982 and 1983.[3] As table 5 shows, all states lost federal support of social services between 1981 and 1983, yet

---

3. Eugene C. Durman, Barbara A. Davis, and Randall R. Bovbjerg, "Block Grants and the New Federalism: The Second Year Experience," Contract Report (Washington, D.C.: Urban Institute, April 1984), p. 6ff.

TABLE 5

FUNDING PROVIDED FOR SOCIAL SERVICES BLOCK GRANTS AND TITLE XX IN EIGHTEEN STATES, FISCAL YEARS 1981–83

Millions of dollars

State	Funding for 1981			Percent Change, 1981–83		
	Title XX (Federal)	Other	Total[a]	Social Service Block Grants	Other	Total
Arizona	32.3	7.5	39.8	−10.2	9.3	−6.5
California	304.6	427.7	732.3	−15.5	16.0	2.9
Colorado	36.1	45.7	81.8	−13.9	16.4	3.1
Florida	100.5	53.4	153.9	−0.7	9.9	3.0
Illinois	147.2	121.7	268.9	−17.0	33.4	5.8
Kentucky	45.2	21.4	66.6	−12.6	68.2	13.3
Massachusetts	78.7	56.1	134.8	−21.6	52.2	9.1
Michigan	115.6	464.8	580.4	−6.6	1.4	−0.2
Minnesota	53.3	96.1	149.4	−17.8	119.6	70.2
Missouri	45.3	16.1	61.4	−7.5	−9.9	−8.1
New Jersey	97.8	53.1	150.9	−19.4	32.6	−1.1
New York	235.8	560.3	796.1	−13.0	39.0	23.6
North Carolina	72.0	28.0	100.0	−10.7	3.6	−7.5
Ohio	142.9	44.5	187.4	−19.2	−10.8	−17.2
Oregon	32.5	28.2	60.7	−5.2	29.8	11.0
Texas	168.9	127.2	296.1	−7.5	33.7	10.2
Vermont	6.4	8.8	15.2	−15.6	40.9	17.1
Virginia	64.8	20.6	85.4	−11.5	−9.2	−11.0

SOURCE: Eugene C. Durman, Barbara A. Davis and Randall R. Bovbjerg, "Block Grants and the New Federalism: The Second Year Experience," Contract Report 3076-01 (Washington, D.C.: Urban Institute, April 1984).

a. Total includes state, local, and other federal funds in addition to block grant or Title XX dollars.

eleven of the eighteen increased total social services funds during that period; nine of these resorted primarily to increased contributions from a state general fund. Even among states that did not fully substitute new dollars for lost ones, all except three made some reduction in the deficit: fifteen of the eighteen states showed a gain in nonfederal block-grant funding for social services between 1981 and 1983. Three states (Kentucky, Minnesota, and Vermont) demonstrated a particularly strong commitment to social services, increasing other resources sufficiently to offset not only the federal block-grant losses but also inflation. (Note, however, that these resources include other federal funds and thus may indicate intertitle and interblock transfers as well as increased local revenues.)

In fiscal 1982 the social services block grant provided 30 percent of the funds for child welfare services in all states (table 6).[4] Funds from largely state and also local and private sources accounted for 53 percent of all child welfare monies. Even if each state distributed its losses in social service funding pro rata among the individual services (which was not the case), children's services would feel fewer negative effects than other social services because of the buffer of state dollars. When one takes account of the positive impact of state replacement efforts discussed above, child welfare services are left with relatively modest losses in nominal funding.

The generally high level of state support for child welfare services indicates that child welfare has relatively high priority among the social services available in most states. In the six states included in The Urban Institute's study of child welfare services, child welfare services were explicitly identified as a top priority. New York offers a good example of a state acting on its priorities: in 1979 the state enacted the Child Welfare Reform Act. A precursor to the federal Adoption Assistance and Child Welfare Act of 1980, the 1979 act contains provisions for cost-sharing to encourage local development of preventive and supportive services and to reduce the need for foster care. The subsequent federal legislation reflected the service priorities of New York and other states and the existing trends in service delivery: foster care was already decreasing (a decline of 52 percent between 1977 and 1982),[5] and prevention programs were in place or being

---

4. Child welfare services are child protective services, foster care, adoption, preventive and supportive in-home care, and day care not related to employment.
5. American Public Welfare Association, *Characteristics of Children in Substitute and Adoptive Care* (Washington, D.C.: APWA, December 1983), p. 16.

developed by 60 percent of the states in 1981.[6] Indeed, most states in 1981 had already gone beyond the requirements of the Adoption Assistance and Child Welfare Act of 1980 in planning for the delivery of child welfare services.[7] The states were clearly not waiting for the federal lead, either in program initiatives or in funding.

Health Services

Many states similarly showed a tendency to replace lost block-grant monies for health services (table 7). The most extensive replacement occurred in the services pertaining to alcohol, drug abuse, and mental health; thirteen states increased total funds, eight of these despite losses of federal block-grant money. Not all states faced decreases in federal funds for such services between fiscal years 1981 and 1983 because of substantial carry-over funds, unspent categorical monies from federal allocations before block grants were awarded. In two states, North Carolina and Texas, the combination of increased federal block-grant funds and increased state funds enabled the states to keep pace with inflation (estimated at 24 percent for medical services during 1981–83).

Mental health is the part of alcohol, drug abuse, and mental health block grant that is perhaps most applicable to children. In general, states had limited flexibility in shifting dollars among mental health, alcoholism, and drug abuse areas, so differences in the rates of funding change among the areas largely reflect the extent of dependence on federal funds before block grants were awarded. Since mental health services are the least dependent on federal support, they generally fared better than alcohol and drug abuse programs. Mental health revenues increased significantly (by more than 10 percent) in three out of eleven states, and increased modestly in five more states; no state saw decreases of more than 2 percent. By contrast, six of twelve states faced large revenue losses (9 percent or more) in drug abuse funds. Funding for alcoholism programs demonstrated the greatest variability across the surveyed states: four states saw increases of 20 percent or more, while three others faced decreases of more than 15 percent.[8]

---

6. Of the fifty-two child welfare plans for fiscal 1982, thirty-one contained preventive services among their goals and objectives. See Madeleine H. Kimmich, "State Child Welfare Program Plans: Service Budgets and Expenditure Reports," Contract Report (Washington, D.C.: Urban Institute, August 1983).

7. Kimmich, "State Child Welfare Program Plans," p. 14ff.

8. Durman, Davis, and Bovbjerg, "Block Grants and the New Federalism," p. 115.

TABLE 6

PERCENT FUNDING PROVIDED FOR CHILD WELFARE SERVICES IN SELECTED STATES, BY VARIOUS SOURCES, FISCAL 1982

State	Thousands of Dollars	Title IV(B)	Title XX	Title IVE(A)	Other Federal	State, Local Private
Alabama[a]	62,186.9	2	59	3	6	12
Arizona	30,569.0	9	1	4	0	86
Arkansas	14,662.2	22	40	4	4	34
California	422,081.7	3	25	13	3	57
Colorado	64,942.8	6	48	1	*	44
Connecticut	35,373.0	3	1	0	*	96
Delaware	7,751.2	4	48	4	1	43
District of Columbia	37,620.0	1	19	3	0	78[b]
Florida	117,524.7	5	41	2	3	49
Georgia	57,044.5	7	33	6	7	48
Idaho	12,097.6	7	62	4	0	26
Illinois	173,702.5	4	52	5	2	37
Indiana	54,635.0	6	34	4	0	56
Iowa	36,626.6	4	39	2	10	44
Kansas	67,337.8	2	17	5	21	54
Kentucky	32,639.0	9	40	6	3	43
Louisiana	63,256.0	7	39	9	3	43
Maine[a]	15,254.9	2	36	16	*	45
Maryland	66,814.0	5	42	5	*	47
Massachusetts	197,682.4	2	32	2	0	64
Michigan[c]	171,556.0	2	17	15	2	63
Minnesota	98,961.0	4	23	5	1	67
Mississippi[a]	25,268.8	5	67	5	0	22
Missouri	53,781.0	8	45	4	*	42
Montana	7,421.0	4	45	8	3	40
Nebraska	17,816.1	6	43	6	3	44

Nevada	11,324.0	4	48	8	*	39
New Hampshire[a]	9,076.4	4	52	6	1	37
New Jersey[a]	142,032.0	1	42	1	4	52
New Mexico[a]	15,908.0	3	48	2	1	45
New York[a]	818,627.0	9	18	17	5	51
North Dakota	28,670.9	4	41	10	11	34
Ohio	152,203.0	4	29	3	2	61
Oklahoma	24,301.8	16	55	*	0	28
Oregon	72,005.6	3	22	6	8	60
Pennsylvania	309,500.0	2	18	8	1	71
Rhode Island	23,109.6	3	4	2	1	91
South Carolina	33,543.0	7	57	3	0	33
South Dakota[a]	8,207.9	9	45	8	13	25
Tennessee	54,224	6	65	5	*	23
Texas[c]	70,387.0	7	48	8	0	36
Utah	11,631.4	11	33	4	11	42
Virgin Islands	3,089.5	7	0	11	3	79
Virginia	48,625.0	8	42	12	1	37
Washington	48,132.9	7	33	4	2	54
West Virginia	36,517.0	7	41	4	4	43
Wisconsin	85,194.0	5	27	15	0	53
Wyoming	13,175.0	3	15	35	2	45
All states	3,964,090.7	5	30	9	3	53

SOURCE: Jeffry J. Koshel and Madeleine H. Kimmich, "Summary Report on the Implementation of P.L. 96-272," Contract Report 3076-04 (Washington, D.C.: Urban Institute, September 1983), table 4, p. 24. Data unavailable for Alaska, Guam, Hawaii, North Carolina, Vermont, and Puerto Rico.

* Less than ½ percent.

a. Data are for fiscal 1981.

b. Seventy-seven percent of this is a direct federal payment to the District of Columbia.

c. Unpublished data. Michigan excludes projected share of central administration costs. Texas excludes fringe benefits.

TABLE 7

FUNDING PROVIDED FOR HEALTH BLOCK GRANTS IN EIGHTEEN STATES, FISCAL YEARS 1981–83

(Millions of dollars)

| | Alcohol, Drug Abuse, Mental Health | | | | Maternal and Child Health | | | | Preventive Health Services | | | |
| | Funding | | Percent Change | | Funding | | Percent Change | | Funding | | Percent Change | |
	Federal Block[a] Grant	Fiscal 1981 Total[b]	Federal Block Grant	Fiscal 1981–83 Total	Federal[c]	Fiscal 1981 Total[d]	Federal	Fiscal 1981–83 Total	Federal[c]	Fiscal 1981 Total[d]	Federal	Fiscal 1981–83 Total
Arizona	9.9	27.6	7.1[e]	44.9	5.1	9.2[f]	−35.3	−15.2	1.1	1.9	0.0	136.8
California	57.3	540.3	−27.7	1.5	23.5	75.7	3.0	17.3	5.7	7.5	57.9[g]	56.0
Colorado	8.4	51.3	2.4	3.5	7.6	14.9	−13.2	−10.7	4.4	8.2	−9.1	15.9
Florida	31.3	90.3	29.7	4.3	13.3	53.8	−21.8	18.2	4.4	10.5	−31.8	2.9
Illinois	...	...	...	...	13.8	27.5	1.4	−2.9	3.0	5.4	−6.7	13.0
Kentucky	5.2	31.8	−34.6	−7.9	6.7	21.8	4.5	12.4	1.5	9.3	−6.7	3.2
Massachusetts	22.4	72.5	−17.4	14.2	9.9	17.1	2.0	3.5	2.6	5.8	−7.7	−6.9
Michigan	11.5	50.7[h]	−2.6	19.5	13.6	34.0	0.0	5.6	4.4	4.9	−6.8	−10.2
Minnesota	...	...	...	...	8.1	11.0	−24.7	−12.7	2.0	2.7	45.0	37.0
Missouri	11.3	20.9	−16.8	1.0	8.4	19.2	−2.4	−10.9	2.0	3.1	−20.0	−16.1
New Jersey	25.9	56.3	−18.5	−3.0	...	...	...	...	...	...	...	19.5
New York[i]	39.1	227.3[h]	−1.8	19.7	30.1	87.2	−1.0	1.0	7.0	8.2	20.0	19.5
North Carolina[i]	12.3	76.2	7.3	26.0	...	...	...	...	...	...	...	...
Ohio	...	...	...	...	...	...	...	...	...	...	...	...
Oregon	4.6	11.8	10.9	7.6	...	...	...	...	...	...	...	...
Texas	22.9	61.4	−4.4	24.1	21.7	43.7[j]	−16.1	31.6	3.7	5.9[k]	24.3	20.3
Vermont	4.4	15.2	−11.4	11.8	1.1	3.4	9.1	41.2	0.6	1.0	−50.0	−20.0
Virginia	8.5	23.0	−9.4	15.7	...	...	...	...	...	...	...	...

Source: Durman, Davis and Bovbjerg, "Block Grants and the New Federalism: The Second Year Experience." Data for preventive health services are from the February 6, 1984, version of the report. All data are on the basis of state fiscal year.

a. Federal blocks include block grant funds plus carry-over funds from categorical programs before block grants were awarded.

b. Total includes, in addition to funds from federal block grants, block-related categorical support such as reimbursements from Title XIX or Title XX, state funds, local funds provided in response to state requirements, and fees and private insurance reimbursements reported to the state.

c. Includes block grant and overlapping funds plus related categorical support.

d. Total includes state funds, local funds provided in response to state requirements, and fee and reimbursement revenues of which the states are aware (for example, Title XIX and private insurers), in addition to federal funds.

e. Fiscal 1983 figures for states include expenditures for federal fiscal 1984 contracts, which inflate apparent 1981–83 growth.

f. Does not include state funds in support of crippled children's services.

g. The large increase reflects forward-funding for emergency medical services from the carry-over such that the state received two years of support in fiscal 1983.

h. Excludes mental health expenditures, which were not consistently reported.

i. Data on maternal and child health funding are for 1982 rather than 1981; the percent change is for 1982–83. This also pertains to data for North Carolina on alcohol, drug abuse, and mental health.

j. Does not include local matching funds.

k. Excludes fee and reimbursement revenues.

In the other two health block grants, states again significantly increased nonfederal revenues to counteract some of the effects of the federal cutbacks. As in the alcohol, drug abuse, and mental health block grant, the federal reductions in maternal and child health were cushioned by significant amounts of carry-over funds from the previous categorical programs. Eight of thirteen states increased total dollars in maternal and child health between fiscal years 1981 and 1983, and three more were able to replace some of the loss in federal funding. Two states, Texas and Vermont, managed to increase maternal and child health funds even beyond inflation, so that they recorded a real expansion of services in this program area.

It is important to recall that state support for block-grant related services for maternal and child health was most often service-specific. Appeals for a particular health need were more likely to be acted upon by deficit-sensitive legislators than were broad requests. For example, Massachusetts passed a special appropriation of $500,000 during fiscal 1983 to maintain Boston's program of maternal and infant care/children and youth services, which had been threatened with severe cutbacks due to state formula changes in the maternal and child health area.

Nine states of thirteen increased total funding for preventive health services between fiscal years 1981 and 1983, with five of these compensating not only for the federal losses but also for inflation (estimated at 14 percent for the two-year period, since most of the funds are used to purchase general goods and services rather than medical services). Only Michigan was unable to replace any of the federal losses and therefore faced declining funds from nonfederal as well as federal sources.

Intertitle and Interblock Transfers

Much of the "replacement" activity examined above included trading losses in a specific block grant with funds from other federal sources. These sources are generally tapped through legal processes called intertitle transfers and interblock transfers. Among children's programs, intertitle transfer is most often used to shift service costs from the social services block grant either to Title IV(A) of AFDC in the case of day care, or to Title XIX (medicaid) in the case of health-related services. The advantage is that Title IV(A) and Title XIX are both entitlement programs with open-ended funding, while the social services block grant has a fixed appropriation level and distribution formula. Intertitle transfer is becoming an increasingly popular strategy for maximizing federal support, more so as federal appropriations for categorical and block grant programs decrease. The General Accounting Office reports that in fiscal 1979 thirteen states transferred $20.8 million in services from Title XX; in the three-year period from fiscal years 1980 to 1982 thirty-one states made transfers worth $73.6 million. Most transfers were to Title XIX; the next largest number went to Title IV(A).[9]

Among the eighteen states surveyed by The Urban Institute, four relied heavily and three others moderately on intertitle transfer to replace federal losses in social services block grants. Intertitle transfers involving the largest amounts of dollars occurred in Texas, New York, and Oregon, where major portions of home care services for the elderly and impaired were transferred to Title XIX.[10] While this program only rarely serves children, the transfer of costs out of social services block grants frees dollars for children's services—as well as for other purposes. A local example illustrates this point: in Boston local health providers redefined their mental health services to be reimbursable under Title XIX; the freed funds from social services block grants reportedly enabled some neighborhood health centers to avoid fee increases.

The use of Title IV(A) child care disregard to support child day care services is a prevalent example of intertitle transfer. The Children's Defense Fund reports that in fiscal 1982 ten states changed completely from social services block grants to day care funding by Title IV(A).[11] Such a shift implicitly tightens eligibility and lowers payment levels because the Title IV(A) child care disregard applies only to AFDC recipients, and reimbursement is limited to $160 a month.

Transfer among sources of funding for child welfare services was made possible through a provision of the Adoption Assistance and Child Welfare Act of 1980 to encourage reductions in foster care. If a state fails to spend (or does not plan to spend) all Title IV(E) foster care funds, it may transfer a limited amount of the Title IV(E) funds to Title IV(B).[12] Fourteen states made such a shift in fiscal 1981, the

---

9. General Accounting Office, "Intertitle Transfers—A Way for States to Increase Federal Funding for Social Services," Report HRD–18–116 (Washington, D.C.: GAO, July 10, 1981).

10. Durman, Davis, and Bovbjerg, "Block Grants and the New Federalism," p. 13.

11. Helen Blank, *Children and Federal Child Care Cuts: A National Survey of the Impact of Federal Title XX Cuts on State Child Care Systems, 1981–1983* (Washington, D.C.: Children's Defense Fund, 1983).

12. Even in years in which Title IV(E) is not capped, the legislation provides for fund transfers.

first year of implementation of the Adoption Assistance and Child Welfare Act.

This act also potentially provides additional Title IV(B) funds when appropriations are above $56 million to states that meet the Section 427 requirements.[13] Thirty-four states became self-certified in fiscal 1981, ten more in fiscal 1982, and five more in fiscal 1983—these forty-nine states thus received a share of the "extra" Title IV(B) monies available in each year.[14] These monies, as well as funds transferred to Title IV(B) from Title IV(E), were designed to enable states to expand or to initiate preventive and restorative services. However, with the reductions in the social services block grants, states generally used these new monies as replacement funds, an easy matter since the two funding sources had long been used together for child welfare services (see table 6 above). For example,

- Michigan redefined its family services to be "preventive services for high-risk families," so that such services would be covered under Title IV(B).
- In Kentucky the Title IV(B) funds were used explicitly to cover child protective services and foster care staff formerly paid from funds provided by the social services block grant; this action left no Title IV(B) funds for new prevention efforts.
- California created its own block grant to be available to the counties; this state consolidated federal funds from the social services block grant, Title IV(B), Title IV(E), child abuse and neglect, and state funds, thus blunting the categorical thrust of the Adoption Assistance and Child Welfare Act.

The states' use of transfers in these ways does not indicate a commitment to any particular service, but rather underlines the need and desire for additional federal funds. By contrast, the other prevalent type of fund transfer among the block grants is a zero-sum game and does, to a certain extent, reflect relative service priorities. The Omnibus Budget Reconciliation Act of 1981, which created the block grants, includes numerous provisions for limited amounts of interblock transfers: social services block grants to or from block grants for low-

---

13. These requirements include a foster care inventory, a foster care information system, a case-review system, and reunification services.

14. Some states subsequently failed to pass review by the Department of Health and Human Services—four in fiscal 1981 and one in fiscal 1982—and other states withdrew from the process—six states in fiscal 1981, three in fiscal 1982, and one in fiscal 1983.

income home energy assistance, transfers from these two types of grants to any of the health block grants, low-income home energy assistance to or from community services block grants, preventive health or alcohol, drug abuse, and mental health to any other health block grant. Community services block-grant funds can also be transferred to Head Start or programs for older Americans.

Among the eighteen states studied, the greatest number (eight) made transfers into social service block grants from block grants for low-income home energy assistance. Several states also transferred funds into the health block grants—five made transfers into maternal and child health and four into preventive health. These health-related transfers were generally small amounts, especially in comparison to the amount of carry-over funds available.

While states are increasingly turning to intertitle and interblock transfers as ways to replace lost federal support for particular children's services, it appears clear that their own revenues are still considered a more fruitful source. State and local governments provide the majority of the funds supporting state child welfare services, and state contributions to health programs appear to be increasing. To the extent that reduced federal funding for the six block grants has affected children's social services, health, and education programs, it is encouraging to note the significant efforts by states to supplement the federal block appropriations with other federal monies and, more important, with state general funds. Social service-related child welfare services and health services in general have been the focus of state replacement efforts, while community service block grants and services resulting from Chapter 2 of the Education Consolidation and Improvement Act have not been appreciably supplemented.

Priorities among Services

From the above discussion it may appear that states have demonstrated a stronger commitment to supplemental funding levels in social services and health services than in other block-grant areas, suggesting that the former services are a higher priority. However, the aggregate nature of the block-grant programs may hide important distinctions among the services included in each block grant. The following paragraphs examine state preferences among the discrete services composing each block grant in order to determine the status of services particularly for children.

Social Services

Most states do place childrens' services high on the list. The ranking is reflected both in the high *level* of state revenues going to child welfare services (table 6) and in the *share* of social services block-grant funds spent on child welfare services. Nineteen states (of forty-seven reviewed) reported in their fiscal 1982 child welfare state plans that federal contributions from social services block grants to state child welfare services amounted to more than half the state's social services block-grant allocation.[15] Many states explicitly make child welfare services a top priority. For example,

- California's three top-priority services include two children's services—child protective services and out-of-home care for children.
- Kentucky lists five high-priority services, including three for children—child protective services, foster care, and adoption services.
- Virginia mandates nine social services block-grant services, including five for children—child protective services, foster care, adoption, day care, and early and periodic screening, diagnosis, and treatment services.

The common factor among states in their social services priorities seems to be the critical nature of services: crisis services are provided before preventive and supportive services; hence child protective services and foster care (as an emergency measure in cases of abuse or neglect) are given high priorities, often accompanied by adult protective services. Texas, for example, made this priorities process very explicit by categorizing all situations needing social services attention as life endangering, safety endangering, or high risk of abuse or neglect. As their funding from social services block grants ran out, Texas officials eliminated services to persons in the last category. In Michigan, the Department of Social Services eliminated support from social services block grants for all services except child protective services, foster care, and adult placement services.

Perhaps more revealing than a state's explicit assertion of service priorities is its allocation of available funds among the competing social services. Larger shares of revenues go to the services that are more important. In the eighteen states surveyed, allocations followed the familiar pattern of crisis services before prevention services. As table

15. Kimmich, "State Child Welfare Program Plans," p. 21.

8 indicates, between fiscal years 1981 and 1983 the states increased resources most often in child protective services (fifteen of seventeen states) and adult protective services (eleven of fifteen states increased funding; two others maintained it at about the same level). Foster care and adoption services also frequently received larger portions of social services dollars (thirteen of seventeen states showed increases). Home-based services similarly did well, increasing allocation shares in eleven of seventeen states. This service category includes some preventive and supportive services for children, but primarily consists of in-home care for the elderly who are at high risk of institutionalization. What appears to be increasing state support for preventive services is rather a focus on high-risk situations (and situations in which there are high alternative costs).

Of the eight groups of services listed in table 8, the only child-specific service to which states generally did not give added support was day care. Seven states devoted a larger share of social services funds to day care, while eleven states reduced their shares. The explanation is that day care is, for the most part, not a crisis service. States generally maintained their support for protective day care, a small part of total spending on day care, while reducing the day care used to facilitate the work or training efforts of low-income clients. Day care is a prime candidate for intertitle transfer—ten states are known to have completely shifted their Title XX day care services to Title IV(A).[16] Whether intertitle transfer means a loss in funds to day care cannot be estimated since figures are not generally available on the amount of money spent under the Title IV(A) child care disregard. In addition, one dollar of Title IV(A) funds may purchase more child care than did one dollar of Title XX, because Title IV(A)-subsidized care is usually a less expensive form of care; the dollar loss from shifting coverage from Title XX to Title IV(A) may not be easily translatable into a loss in the amount of day care (although the quality-quantity trade-off cannot be denied). Texas offers an example of such a quality-quantity trade-off in day care supported by the social services block-grant: while block-grant expenditures for day care decreased between fiscal years 1981 and 1983, the actual number of day care slots increased during the same period. This is attributable largely to the reduction in federal requirements, which enabled the centers to increase staff-child ratios and the state to decrease daily reimbursement rates.[17]

---

16. Blank, *Children and Federal Child Care Cuts,* p. 7.
17. Durman, Davis, and Bovbjerg, "Block Grants and the New Federalism," p. 25ff.

TABLE 8

DISTRIBUTION OF EIGHTEEN STATES' TOTAL SOCIAL SERVICES SPENDING IN FISCAL 1981 AMONG CHILDREN'S PROGRAMS AND CHANGE IN PROPORTION ALLOCATED IN FISCAL YEARS 1981–83[a]

(Percent)

| State | Adoption and Foster Care | | Children's Day Care | | Protective Services | | | |
| | | | | | Children | | Adults | |
	State's 1981 Distribution	Percent Change 1981–83	State's 1981 Distribution	Percent Change 1981–83	State's 1981 Distribution	Percent Change 1981–83	State's 1981 Distribution	Percent Change 1981–83
Arizona	14.1	14.2	16.3	12.3	2.1	309.5	2.9	37.9
California	2.3	8.7	29.6	−0.7	n.a.	n.a.	n.a.	n.a.
Colorado	31.3	5.4	21.9	−30.6[b]	31.7	15.8	3.4	23.5
Florida	4.9	32.7	14.1	41.8	14.1	27.7	6.6	12.1
Illinois	6.3	9.5	15.1	5.3	1.8	72.2	1.4	100.0
Kentucky	9.7	29.9	6.3	11.1	8.1	127.2	3.8	84.2
Massachusetts	2.1	123.8	26.2	3.8	2.1	4.8	0.7	100.0
Michigan	20.0	−2.5	5.3	−50.9[c]	3.4	26.5	0.3	0.0
Minnesota	6.5	69.2	7.2	−36.1	8.3	−36.1	1.4	−50.0
Missouri	n.a.	n.a.	19.4	−15.5	29.8	32.9	n.a.	n.a.
New Jersey	3.9	48.7	24.4	1.2	7.8	42.3	1.3	130.8
New York	15.0	−11.3	20.0	−14.5	6.6	−18.2	1.5	0.0
North Carolina[d]	5.8	84.5	14.7	12.2	4.9	89.8	1.0	100.0
Ohio	7.8	10.3	17.1	−18.7	6.8	69.1	2.4	50.0
Oregon	25.0	−7.6	2.8	−21.4	10.2	5.9	n.a.	n.a.
Texas	5.8	−12.1	14.8	−23.6	18.1	24.3	7.5	13.3
Vermont	42.7	44.1	12.5	−35.2	3.0	3.3	7.9	−41.6[e]
Virginia	15.5	74.2	13.6	−33.1	9.6	49.0	1.0	190.0

TABLE 8 (Continued)

State	Home-Based Services State's 1981 Distribution	Home-Based Services Percent Change 1981–83	Employment, Education, and Training State's 1981 Distribution	Employment, Education, and Training Percent Change 1981–83	Family Planning State's 1981 Distribution	Family Planning Percent Change 1981–83	Information and Referral and Other Services State's 1981 Distribution	Information and Referral and Other Services Percent Change 1981–83
Arizona	7.5	50.7	13.6	−27.2	0.8	0.0	29.9	−45.2
California	35.9	−2.5	0.0	...	4.1	34.1	28.0	−2.9
Colorado	6.8	−25.0	0.0	...	0.0	...	0.0	n.a.
Florida	4.2	−35.7	2.1	...	3.5	14.3	50.5	−18.4
Illinois	10.8	5.6	4.3	39.5	1.3	−23.1	59.0	−9.8
Kentucky	4.7	91.5	0.4	−100.0	0.0	...	67.1	−31.3
Massachusetts	4.5	17.8	0.0	...	0.7	28.6	36.7	−13.1
Michigan	10.4	12.5	1.8	83.3	0.0	...	51.4	−0.8
Minnesota	6.2	−17.7	1.5	26.7	0.2	0.0	67.0	31.2
Missouri	n.a.	n.a.	n.a.	n.a.	n.a.	n.a.	34.2	−8.5
New Jersey	11.3	−8.8	1.5	26.7	2.0	−25.0	46.9	−4.9
New York	43.6	21.8	0.3	133.3	2.3	13.0	10.3	−42.7
North Carolina[d]	13.3	28.6	0.3	66.7	4.9	−14.3	47.6	−16.0
Ohio	9.5	40.0	7.3	−19.2	1.2	8.3	47.9	−12.1
Oregon	28.8	22.6	0.0	...	0.0	...	15.8	55.1
Texas	27.7	7.2	4.4	4.5	7.4	−14.9	7.1	−18.3
Vermont	3.3	6.3	n.a.	n.a.	0.7	83.3	17.7	−42.5
Virginia	11.0	2.7	8.8	−25.0	5.7	−63.2	33.9	−22.1

SOURCE: Durman, Davis, and Bovbjerg, "Block Grants and the New Federalism: The Second Year Experience."

n.a. Not available.

a. Data for fiscal years 1981 and 1983 are the percent share of the total service dollars spent on a particular service. The percent change is the change in the budget share allocated to a particular service.

b. Day care spending in Colorado may be underestimated because the shift of day care to an income disregard under Title IV(A) could not be measured.

c. Includes Michigan's estimates of increased spending under Title IV(A).

d. Includes federal Title XX funds only.

e. Reflects a change in the definition of a service rather than a program change.

The greater emphasis on crisis services rather than preventive services does not mean that prevention activities were uniformly ignored by states. On the contrary, the potential for states to receive federal funds by implementing the Adoption Assistance and Child Welfare Act appears to have been a strong factor in persuading states to develop preventive services programs or to continue them where they were already begun. California specifically initiated four new services (family reunification services and permanent placement in 1982, family maintenance services and preplacement services in 1983) at the state level, to bring its child welfare services program into compliance with the 1980 act. However, because California has a county-administered system and because of recent state legislation, counties are not required to implement the new services unless sufficient state funds are provided. Indeed, during 1981–82 most California counties acted not in response to the new state service initiatives but in response to the reduction in social services block-grant funds.[18] In general, their decision was to reduce preventive services in order to maintain crisis services. One notable exception was the San Diego County Department of Social Services, which attempted to continue its prevention focus by early intervention in high-risk situations to reduce the need for foster care. The department planned to use the $850,000 saved by this process to expand their reunification services; however, the county board of supervisors expropriated the funds, dealing a severe blow to both the morale and the service delivery system. After this unsuccessful attempt to use foster care offsets to expand preventive services, the department was forced to make numerous changes in its service offerings. It reduced crisis intervention services to children in all but the most severe and immediately life-threatening situations; reduced support services to foster parents; and eliminated its new child sexual abuse treatment team.

Numerous states predate the Adoption Assistance and Child Welfare Act in their commitment to provide preventive services for children. For example,

- As noted above, in 1979 New York statutorily acknowledged the importance—and gave substantial fiscal backing to—preventive services.
- Oregon has similarly long embraced preventive and restorative services, and has supported unusual early intervention programs

18. California Department of Social Services, "Title XX Block Grant: A Report on the Effects of P.L. 97–35 on California Social Services Programs" (California DSS, July 1982).

from offsets to foster care. In the face of cuts in social services block grants, Oregon stubbornly continued its prevention focus: preventive services in fiscal years 1982 and 1983 commanded 38 percent of the Children's Services Division's budget.[19]

- Michigan, despite its high unemployment rate and the severity of the recession overall, sought to support prevention efforts through an unusual tax refund mechanism: taxpayers have the option to designate a portion of their state tax refund for the Children's Trust Fund, with the monies used to support innovative prevention programs for high-risk families. State officials anticipate as much as $20 million per year will be earmarked.[20]
- Massachusetts has similarly attempted to adhere to the spirit of the 1980 act without establishing additional state revenues and without the advantage of receiving a share of the "extra" Title IV(B) funds (Massachusetts withdrew its self-certification for Section 427 in fiscal years 1981–83). The Department of Social Services targeted all children's out-of-home care for the largest cuts in social services funds. However, without having restorative and supportive services available to clients, the department staff found it difficult to contribute to the success of the reunification efforts. Placements rose again in fiscal 1983, many of which were placements for a second or subsequent time, suggesting that too much pressure had been put on the staff to return children to their homes.

Health Services

While children's services generally fared well in competition with other social services, state priorities among health services do not show as clear a pattern by age group. Shifts in state priorities took place largely in the second year of the block grants. The funding reductions in the first year were cushioned by large amounts of carry-over funds; in addition, states had little time to plan, federal funding levels were uncertain, and there were more pressing problems to address, such as shortfalls in the general fund and the changes in AFDC and medicaid. The reductions that states had to make in fiscal 1982 were usually made pro rata; intrablock service priorities appeared more in subsequent years.

---

19. Jeffrey J. Koshel and Madeleine H. Kimmich, "State Child Welfare Services and Federal Legislation: Final Report," Contract Report (Washington, D.C.: Urban Institute, September 1983), p. 72.

20. Ibid., pp. 45, 51.

In fiscal 1983 the states began asserting their own priorities among the services consolidated into each of the three block grants. In the block grant for maternal and child health all services directly or indirectly benefit children; there is no explicit targeting to children versus other age groups. However, state preferences do apear to follow a pattern (see table 9), with maternal and child health services and crippled children's services (from the old Title V programs) receiving equal or greater funds in fiscal 1983 than in fiscal 1981. In nine of thirteen states surveyed, maternal and child health services maintained or increased their funding level; in eight of thirteen states crippled children's services similarly held even or expanded their funding. The deciding factors in states' priorities for maternal and child health appear to be a long history of federal, state, and local

TABLE 9

MATERNAL AND CHILD HEALTH PROGRAMS THAT GAINED FUNDS,
FISCAL YEARS 1981–83

	Total Program Expenditures in 1981 ($ Millions)		Percent Change, 1981–1983	
State	Crippled Children's Services	Maternal and Child Health Services (Title V)	Crippled Children's Services	Maternal and Child Health Services (Title V)
Arizona	0.9	7.9	0.0	−16.5
California	50.9	21.6	15.1	10.6
Colorado	4.3	9.5	−11.6	−14.7
Florida	24.7	26.4	37.2	7.6
Illinois	13.8	12.4	−0.7	2.4
Kentucky	5.9	14.6	18.6	7.5
Massachusetts	4.5	9.2	31.1	−7.6
Michigan	21.5	10.6	4.7	0.0
Minnesota	5.4	5.0	−33.3	14.0
Missouri	8.0	9.9	−6.3	−8.1
New Jersey	. . .	. . .	. . .	. . .
New York[a]	18.6	59.3	−15.1	6.9
North Carolina	. . .	. . .	. . .	. . .
Ohio	. . .	. . .	. . .	. . .
Oregon	. . .	. . .	. . .	. . .
Texas[b]	24.1	16.1	44.8	6.2
Vermont	0.6	2.5	50.0	48.0
Virginia	. . .	. . .	. . .	. . .

SOURCE: Durman, Davis, and Bovbjerg, "Block Grants and the New Federalism: The Second Year Experience."
a. Data for 1981 reflect the state fiscal year 1982 (April 1981–March 1982).
b. Does not include local matching.

TABLE 10

MATERNAL AND CHILD HEALTH PROGRAMS THAT LOST FUNDS,
FISCAL YEARS 1981–83

State	Total Program Expenditures in 1981 ($ Millions)[a]			Percent Change, 1981–83[b]		
	Lead-Based Paint	Sudden Infant Death Syndrome	Adolescent Pregnancy	Lead-Based Paint	Sudden Infant Death Syndrome	Adolescent Pregnancy
Arizona	0.0	0.0	0.0	. . .	. . .	. . .
California	0.3	0.2	0.1	−100.0	−100.0	1203.3
Colorado	0.0	0.1	0.0	. . .	−35.1	c
Florida	0.0	0.1	0.6	. . .	−17.9	−7.0
Illinois	0.9	0.2	0.2	−73.2	−69.4	−100.0
Kentucky	0.3	0.1	0.0	−41.6	−35.5	. . .
Massachusetts	1.9	0.1	0.4	−56.2	31.7	50.6
Michigan	0.6	0.0	0.3	−18.1	728.6	−36.3
Minnesota	0.0	0.1	0.3	. . .	−98.6	−100.0
Missouri	0.6	0.1	0.2	−100.0	8.8	−100.0
New Jersey	. . .	. . .	. . .	. . .	. . .	. . .
New York[a]	3.4	0.3	1.2	−46.9	−70.0	−7.1
North Carolina	. . .	. . .	. . .	. . .	. . .	. . .
Ohio	. . .	. . .	. . .	. . .	. . .	. . .
Oregon	. . .	. . .	. . .	. . .	. . .	. . .
Texas[b]	0.1	0.2	0.5	−100.0	−100.0	−54.3
Vermont	0.0	0.2	0.1	0.0	15.0	31.4
Virginia	. . .	. . .	. . .	. . .	. . .	. . .

SOURCE: Durman, Davis, and Bovbjerg, "Block Grants and the New Federalism: The Second Year Experience."
a. Includes funding from 15 percent federal set-aside.
b. Percentages calculated from unrounded data.
c. Funding increased to $0.05 million in 1983.

collaboration in provision of fairly direct treatment services, rather than contractual service provision or preventive services.[21]

By contrast, the other former categorical programs in the maternal and child health block grant generally lost ground (table 10). Lead-based paint poisoning lost funds in all eight of the states that had programs, with three of those programs being completely eliminated. Eight of eleven states decreased total funding for adolescent pregnancy services. Eight of eleven states decreased support for programs to prevent sudden infant death syndrome. These three types of services

21. Durman, Davis, and Bovbjerg, "Block Grants and the New Federalism," p. 76.

are generally narrowly focused programs with small constituencies. States are more likely to increase support for the more broadly recognized and utilized services formerly funded by Title V—that is, maternal and child health services and crippled children's services. California offers a clear example of such priorities: the state explicitly placed a high priority on perinatal services and high-risk infant follow-up and urged that all maternal and child health contracts be comprehensive, providing a whole year of preventive services. At the same time, the state eliminated all maternal and child health block-grant support for lead-based paint poisoning programs and programs to prevent sudden infant death syndrome.

Similar choices were made at the local level. For example,

- The Wayne County (Detroit) health department eliminated all field services, including public health nurse visits, and reduced the amount of rat control, lead-based paint poisoning, and other special services at county health clinics.
- In Richmond, Virginia, losses in maternal and child health funding forced the city health department to reduce preventive services like dental visits and health education, and to eliminate the childhood lead poisoning control project. The responsibility for lead-based paint poisoning was shifted to general health department staff. In addition, the city maternal and child health program began sharing the nutrition resources of the WIC program (supplemental food program for women, infants, and children). These changes occurred despite an explicit city mandate for maternal and child health services.

Although maternal and child health services and crippled children's services did well relative to lead-based paint poisoning, sudden infant death syndrome, and adolescent pregnancy services, they still did not escape erosion due to inflation. In inflation-adjusted terms only four states registered real increases (over 24 percent for fiscal years 1981–83) in crippled children's services, and only one did so in maternal and child health services.

A similar pattern appears in the preventive services block grant, with states generally supporting services previously administered at the state level and directed at a larger and more geographically diverse population. As in maternal and child health, there is no clear mandate regarding child-focused services because all the preventive health services are fairly equally beneficial to children (although maternal and child health services are, by definition, more narrowly directed toward children than are the block grant preventive health services). Table 11

TABLE 11

STATE PROGRAMMATIC PRIORITIES IN PREVENTIVE HEALTH BLOCK GRANTS,
FISCAL YEARS 1981–83

Program	Status before Block Grants	Number of States Indicating Priority Type[a]			States with Program
		High Priority	*Middle Priority*	*Low Priority*	
Fluoridation	Federal to state (service-specific)	8	6	2	16
Hypertension	Federal to state (service-specific)	10	2	6	18
Health education and risk reduction	Federal to state (service-specific)	7	2	9	18
Health incentive grant, 314(d)	Federal to state (block grant)	9	2	7	18
Emergency medical services	Federal to local (service-specific)	5	2	11	18
Home health	Federal to local	1	0	7	8
Rat control	Federal to local	0	2	9	11

SOURCE: Durman, Davis, and Bovbjerg, "Block Grants and the New Federalism: The Second Year Experience." The table is based on expenditures and interviews.

a. High priority is defined for states with complete expenditure data as a 10 percent or more nominal increase in total spending in the program area (thirteen states). For the five states without complete data, high priority is taken as explicit mention of the area as a high priority. Middle priority is defined for states with complete expenditure data as a total expenditures change for fiscal years 1981–83 of less than plus or minus 10 percent. For states without expenditure data, moderate priority was assigned to programs neither singled out as a high priority nor discussed as an object of cutbacks. Low priority is defined for states with complete expenditure data as a reduction in total spending for fiscal 1981–83 greater than 10 percent. For other states, low priority required specific mention of program reductions.

summarizes the priorities of the eighteen survey states among the preventive health programs. In general states seem to prefer the categorical programs they previously controlled: half or more states gave high priority to hypertension, 314(d), and fluoridation; all were previously federal-to-state programs. By contrast, half or more of the states gave low priority to emergency medical services, home health, and rat control; all were previously federal-to-local programs. The exception is the health education and risk reduction program, which was previously a federal-to-state effort; it appears to be more often a low priority than a high one, but in fact several states have kept the program operating by incorporating it into broader preventive health programs, which the states fund through local health departments.

In sharp contrast to the flexibility built into the maternal and child health and preventive health block grants, the alcohol, drug abuse, and mental health block grant gave states relatively little discretion over service allocations within the block grant. The 5 percent of funding that was not earmarked generally was split pro rata or was used to compensate whichever of the three areas—alcoholism, drug abuse, and mental health—had suffered most from the federal funding requirements. Among the three areas, mental health funds were the least flexible because of the federal requirement to continue funds to all community mental health centers (except those in their last year of developmental funding); each center generally received a pro rata share of the cutbacks. In alcoholism and drug abuse, there was an apparent shift toward prevention and away from treatment services; however, this was largely due to federal earmarking on alcohol and drug abuse prevention efforts. In fact, despite the earmarking, most states were able to maintain existing levels of treatment services by shifting treatment costs to state funding or by redefining the treatment program to fit a "prevention" definition.[22]

Medicaid

As in the health block grants, changes mandated by the Omnibus Budget Reconciliation Act in the medicaid program gave the states added discretion over both service offerings and payment mechanisms.[23] Many states began offering varying amounts of services to the different categories of medically needy eligibles as a way of better targeting optional services they offered. States also began charging copayments for optional services, something that has always been allowed but had been rarely used before the reconciliation act changes. With reduced federal cost sharing, states generally sought to reduce their optional service offerings; most maintained the coverage for major optional services like intermediate care facilities for the mentally retarded, but restricted coverage for minor optional services like dental, optometry, and chiropractor services.

Education

States generally expressed their service preferences for education implicitly through relative funding levels for various programs. State

---

22. Ibid., p. 115.
23. Randall R. Bovbjerg and John Holahan, *Medicaid in the Reagan Era: Federal Policy and State Choices* (Washington, D.C.: Urban Institute Press, 1982).

aid to education has increased significantly in the past decade and has focused increasingly on target groups and on improving jurisdictional equity. All states contribute to special education programs; twenty-two fund bilingual education programs; sixteen have a state-supported categorical program of compensatory education; and eight distribute their general education aid by taking into account each district's disadvantaged school-age population.

Against this backdrop of state support for a variety of education programs, changes brought about by the shift from the Elementary and Secondary Education Act to the Education Consolidation and Improvement Act, coupled with the binding effects of the recession in many states, have generally led to reductions in state support for compensatory education and bilingual education and reductions in the rate of increase in state funding for special education. The states' preference for special education appears to be state mandated, more often legislated for special education or bilingual education than for broader education services for the disadvantaged.[24]

At the local level the decisions about how to spend Education Consolidation and Improvement Act funds were largely proscribed by law; local school districts in the four metropolitan areas studied reduced their support in general for compensatory education (Chapter 1 programs), and certain Chapter 2 programs like follow-through and desegregation programs. In the latter case, local districts showed a tendency to avoid sustaining the old desegregation programs affected by the Emergency School Aid Act even when, as in San Diego, there existed a 65 percent hold-harmless clause for districts (county funding to districts was required to be at least 65 percent of previous year's funding); the limited funds were used instead for basic skills improvement programs.

Employment

All programs in employment were severely cut at the federal level, especially youth programs. In place of numerous categorical youth programs under the Comprehensive Employment and Training Act, the Job Training Partnership Act simply requires that 40 percent of the training money be spent for youth, without any requirement for developing youth-targeted programs. In general this has meant fewer and smaller employment and training programs directed toward youth

---

24. Margaret Simms, "The Impact of Changes in Federal Elementary and Secondary Education Policy," CDP Discussion Paper (Washington, D.C.: Urban Institute, September 1984).

and no replacement for the former youth demonstration programs. Massachusetts is one state that took deliberate action to replace the lost demonstration funds: when it lost its funding for a training program for dropouts, it shifted a school-based program to state funding and used the freed-up Job Training Partnership Act discretionary funds to continue the dropout program. Massachusetts generally showed substantial support for employment and training programs, by increasing state funding for AFDC employment and developing innovative services for use in the work incentive program. Implementation of these new programs has been slow in Massachusetts because it is part of a major change in state AFDC policy under the Dukakis administration.[25]

At the local level the employment and training programs appeared to operate under the same principle that governed the social services and health programs: provide the most necessary services first. This meant continuing to offer training and placement services for employment and eliminating most support services. Indeed, such a pattern was fostered by the funding limitations inherent in the Job Training Partnership Act programs—15 percent for administration and 15 percent for support services. Consequently,

- Boston decreased funding for support services in job training contracts, with an emphasis on provision of placement-only services before any counseling or even training services. (By contrast, the state gave substantial funding to the work incentive program, enabling agencies to offer innovative services.)
- Detroit reduced individual counseling services, testing, and client assessments.
- San Diego reduced outreach services and special services for the disadvantaged.

Summary

Overall the states and localities have demonstrated strong preferences among the groups of services included in the federal block grants and other programs offering services to children. In the social services, crisis needs are met before prevention needs, although the Adoption Assistance and Child Welfare Act has exerted some countervailing pressure and created more balanced services offerings for children. Health services funding appears to favor programs that have

---

25. Demetra Nightingale, "Federal Employment and Training Policy Changes during the Reagan Administration: State and Local Responses," CDP Discussion Paper (Washington, D.C.: Urban Institute, March 1985).

broad geographic scope and address high-incidence problems. Such a focus is not explicitly directed toward children but concentrates on providing basic health coverage at the expense of special programs like lead-based paint poisoning, sudden infant death syndrome, or rat control. Shifts in medicaid funding have potentially worsened the health care situation for families by reducing optional services and increasing copayments. In education and employment, less popular services (those with smaller constituencies) are again the ones to suffer relatively more, with states decreasing support of compensatory education for the disadvantaged and youth training programs.

Devolution of Responsibility to Local Government

The states expressed their commitment to children's services through their efforts to replace lost federal dollars, through explicit service priorities set in legislative mandates, and through the way they distributed funding reductions among competing service programs. Whether or not a state chose to take any of these priority-setting actions, it often also passed along such decisions to local governments. The devolution of responsibility was sometimes very narrowly focused, designed to achieve particular cost-savings—such as Michigan's shift of 25 percent of the costs of AFDC foster care to its counties. In other cases the states used small block grants and passed to the local government reduced funds in a lump sum, with varying amounts of local discretion in distributing the cutbacks.

The more narrow type of devolution of responsibility occurred in a variety of ways. States sometimes passively shifted the financial burden, as when California did not reimburse local districts for the full costs of special education for identified children according to the Education for All Handicapped Children Act; or when Michigan failed to provide matching funds of 50 percent (produced only 16 percent) for local health services. More often the costs were clearly passed along, in advance, to local governments. For example,

- Florida increased the local matching rate for maternal and child health funds (the only one of eighteen states to do so).
- New York transferred funds for low-income home energy assistance, unmatched, to social services block grants, then made the counties match those funds as they did other social services grant monies.
- California shifted to the counties 30 percent of the costs of

health care for the medically indigent (since 1971 the program has been completely state funded).

Devolution of responsibility to local governments also may mean a transfer of broad decision-making responsibility, as when the state allocates funds to counties using a block grant. Among the eighteen states surveyed here several turned to small block grants even when they had replaced some of the lost federal funds, which suggests that devolution is not used simply to pass along funding difficulties.

In the social services area, the states also used small block grants to disperse monies from both social services and community services block grants. California consolidated funding from its general fund and from numerous related federal sources (social services block grants, Title IV(B), Title IV(E), and child abuse and neglect) into a small block grant, then mandated that the reduction be distributed pro rata between an in-home supportive services program and a program to encompass other county social services. The state then left to the counties the decision of how to distribute the cutbacks among the services included in the broad program group (for example, child welfare services, adult and family services, emergency response, and so on). Minnesota similarly gave social services block-grant funds to local governments through a block-grant mechanism, although the design and impetus for that system predated the reconciliation act. In disbursing community services block-grant monies several states began allocating funds directly to counties in an attempt to improve the statewide coverage of the services under the community action program. In most cases the state retained control over the process of designating eligible recipients, so the counties gained little distributional power. A notable exception was Colorado, where counties decided how to allocate the reduced funds from community services block grants among the competing grantees in the community action program.

The practice of passing along block-grant funds from states to local communities was also popular in the health block grants. Five states created small block grants for at least some of their maternal and child health funds. Oregon passed such funds to counties who were free to use them to meet local priorities, without any requirement of state approval of the chosen projects. Missouri combined funds for maternal and child health (Title V) services and lead-based paint poisoning in its awards to all counties; Ohio similarly consolidated all categories that existed before block grants into two basic maternal and child health block-grant programs and distributed the funds to counties. In New York City one agency in the private sector received a lump sum from the state to provide all maternal and child health services for the city.

Similarly in preventive health, five states gave greater discretion to counties by adopting the funding distribution previously used under the health incentive grants program, 314(d), the only preventive services categorical program that was formula-determined. Each state consolidated different combinations of the previously existing categorical programs: Oregon and New York consolidated all that were permitted (federal conditions were put on services such as hypertension and emergency medical); Ohio, North Carolina, and Texas combined health incentive grants, 314(d), with two other services.

Unlike the devolution from state to local government, shifting responsibility from the local government to the private sector—another result of reduced federal funding, but one only briefly discussed here— is neither systematic nor legally binding on private agencies; the action is better characterized as an appeal to private interests. In some cases it works, as when the United Way of Greater Richmond, Virginia, began supporting a number of day care programs whose funding was cut by the Richmond Department of Social Services. However, the private sector has also been adversely affected by Reagan administration cuts in social programs and cannot come to the rescue of all the services that need help. This issue is addressed in more detail in chapter 4.

Changing Distributional Formulas

States transferred programmatic and fiscal responsibility to local governments not only to seek relief from some tough decisions on service reductions, but often also to promote the goal of greater geographic equity. Before implementation of the block grants, few federal categorical programs uniformly supported services in all regions of a state. Often states were bypassed altogether because funds went directly from a federal agency to a local public or private grantee; even when funds did flow through the state government, the restrictions on eligible grantees were such that states could not use the funds to ensure statewide service availability. As states began to exercise their new-found flexibility under the health and social services block grants, they turned frequently to formulas to disperse funds to all their local jurisdictions. In some cases a state may have altered the existing service distribution in order to correct for past inequities; in other cases a state may have embraced a formula distribution to pass on federal cuts pro rata among local jurisdictions, essentially retaining the existing resource shares. Whatever the particular action chosen, the goal was generally to improve statewide service coverage.

Social Services

To distribute social services block-grant funds some states adopted new formulas to more equitably spread the cutbacks among all local jurisdictions. Although the predecessor program, Title XX, was already a modified block grant, the states were forced to deal anew with distributional issues because of the depth of the funding reductions. For example,

- Minnesota responded to local government complaints about geographic equity by altering its allocation formula for socials services block-grant funds to correspond more closely to population distribution. However, it additionally "held harmless" the existing grantees, so as social services block-grant resources diminished rather than expanded, little real change occurred.
- New Jersey counties argued strongly about the best factors for the state to include in the social services block-grant distribution formulas. An AFDC population factor favored the northern counties; a low-income population factor favored the southern ones; and the state eventually negotiated a compromise.
- Virginia altered its allocation of social services block-grant funds by adding one factor (the public assistance population), changing another factor (determination of caseload measures), and retaining one factor from the previous allocation formula (overall population).
- California made a modest reallocation toward small rural areas, with little resistance from the large counties because there were relatively few dollars at stake.

Much more extensive were the efforts to change the distribution of funds from community services block grants. Sixteen of the eighteen states studied were concerned about achieving statewide coverage for services, which they did not have earlier under the community action program. As noted above, several states distributed community services block-grant funds to counties and then to the community action programs as a way to persuade the community action program agencies to expand their services to geographic areas not previously covered. Other methods were used to create a statewide network of services provided by the community action program: for example, Virginia claimed less than the allowable 5 percent for administration and used the remainder for service expansion; Oregon and New York used the 5 percent discretionary money for extra service coverage; and several states persuaded existing community action agencies to subcontract to a new agency in a previously unserved location.

Underlying the desires of many states to create a statewide network of services was their awareness of the need for allocating resources according to the relative incidence of poverty within a state. Community Service Administration awards (part of the Department of Health and Human Services) were purported to reflect poverty levels but were not always sensitive to the variations within a state, only between states. With implementation of community services block grants fourteen of the eighteen surveyed states changed the basis of their local allocations from historical patterns under the Community Services Administration to local poverty levels. In general this change meant a reallocation of funds from big city community action program agencies to rural community action programs—for example, Detroit, Los Angeles, and Chicago received smaller shares of community services block-grant funds than they had received under Community Services Administration. A few states made abrupt formula changes—Arizona abandoned a 1982 formula that was calculated according to historical levels of expenditures to a 1983 formula based completely on poverty. More often states considered multiple factors to cushion the effects of changes in formulas on previously favored recipients.

Health Services

Numerous states made changes in their distribution formulas for health block grants, often to address issues of geographic equity. Eight of eighteen states changed the county shares when disbursing maternal and child health funds. Three states increased categorical funding to low-funded, usually nonmetropolitan counties. Three other states modified the distribution formula so that every county received some maternal and child health monies. (Oregon added to its formula two factors, measures for need and density; Missouri shifted to general contracts by formula instead of competitive purchase of service.) Massachusetts built a careful case for its changes: it conducted a statewide needs assessment for maternal and child health and for WIC services (supplemental food program for women, infants, and children), then reallocated these funds according to local needs. In both cases urban areas, especially Boston, were found to be receiving an unnecessarily large share, so the decision was made to reduce shares gradually over a few years.

Similarly, seven of eighteen states altered or plan to alter their formulas to achieve wider geographic impact in the distribution of preventive health funds, so that there has been a general shift toward rural areas and away from urban areas. Most of these states created small block grants and distributed the funds per capita, but a few states such as Texas adopted the old 314(d) formula, which also tended to favor rural areas.

States have significantly less distributional flexibility under the block grant for alcohol, drug abuse, and mental health than under the other health blocks because of the requirement that existing community mental health centers have to be funded (unless they are in their last year of federal seed-money support). However, any funds left after the requirement was met were state-discretionary. Minnesota allocated these remaining mental health funds to all its counties (using the state's formula for distributing its mental health funds); community mental health centers could compete locally for a share of these discretionary monies.

Education

Under the education block grant (Chapter 2 of the Education Consolidation and Improvement Act), federal Chapter 2 funds were distributed to states based on their student-aged population. This led to some interstate redistribution toward small and rural states, away from larger and more urban ones. In allocating to school districts the states had the option of using additional factors, such as the special needs of students or of districts, to cushion the blow to districts hurt especially by cuts in Title I (Chapter 1) and elimination of the Emergency School Aid Act of 1972—generally urban districts more than suburban ones. In 1982–83, the first year of Chapter 2, eighteen states used student enrollment as the basis for distributing 80 percent or more of their Chapter 2 funds; only three states based allocation of Chapter 2 monies on race or the existence of a desegregation program, although many states tried to help districts formerly designated for assistance under the Emergency School Aid Act by relying on "hold-harmless" clauses or by considering student socioeconomic status as a factor.[26]

---

26. Simms, "Impact of Changes in Federal Elementary and Secondary Education Policy."

Other Cost-Cutting Efforts

While most of the strategies examined above seem to reflect broad philosophies of the states—that certain services are more important than others, that statewide service availability is desirable, and so on—states have also taken a broad range of actions for the purpose of cutting specific costs. When resources are limited, any attempt to help one particular recipient group or to expand one service explicitly means disadvantages for another needy group or another service. States have had to make hard choices about how to respond to changing federal rules and reduced federal financial participation. Program-specific changes made by states are of three types: changes in eligibility, service coverage, and payments.

Changes in Eligibility

The most significant eligibility changes affecting children made by the Reagan administration were in the AFDC program. The federal regulatory changes particularly hurt the working poor through changes in income limits, work requirements, and benefit levels. Many states sought to reduce their matching costs by not raising the AFDC payment standard to keep up with inflation, and the effect was to further tighten eligibility for working people because even small increases in wage levels would put them above AFDC eligibility levels.

Tighter AFDC eligibility directly affects medicaid recipients, since in all states AFDC recipients are automatically eligible for medicaid. Most states did not directly limit medicaid eligibility because it would simply mean shifting costs to state- or county-funded medical insurance programs. States did, however, make selective eligibility restrictions, targeting optional services to some portions of the medically needy (children, for example, could receive such services).

Eligibility for maternal and child health services was similarly limited in some states. Three of eighteen states surveyed restricted eligibility for crippled children's services by reducing the age limit or by not raising the income eligibility ceiling with inflation. In mental health, a few states took a positive approach by requiring community mental health centers to serve the chronically ill first.

Federal requirements pertaining to recipients of social services block grants were eliminated. No longer do half the social services block-grant recipients have to be welfare recipients. This regulatory change had the potential of drastically reducing services to AFDC eligibles, but states appear to have retained their commitment to the most needy. As Durman, Davis, and Bovbjerg observe, the end of the 50 percent rule in social services block grants "does not seem to have resulted in a shift away from a low-income, high-need target population. The general trend in the states was to lower eligibility standards, i.e. to serve a relatively poor or 'needier' population, or to leave eligibility unchanged, as they adjusted to a lower overall level of federal support."[27]

The retention of services for the most needy often came at the expense of the marginal, working poor. A good example is day care services. Because it is generally not a crisis-oriented service, day care often received a large share of the cuts in social services block grants (see table 8 above). However, increasing AFDC work requirements led to the need for employment-related day care services. Ten states shifted completely from social services block grants to Title IV(A) to fund child care, but this meant an eligibility change—non-AFDC recipients who had received Title XX day care services no longer had any access to subsidized day care. Even in states that continued to use social services block-grant funds for day care, restrictions were greater than before. In Virginia, for example, centers and homes were required to limit their poor participants to half of those served in an attempt to make providers less dependent on public funds; and the state only subsidized the AFDC-eligible children.

Some local jurisdictions took similar actions: the Richmond Department of Social Services restricted its day care services to currently eligible recipients of AFDC, eliminating the service for the large group of income eligibles (by Title XX definitions) and former recipients of AFDC. In Michigan the supply of subsidized day care became an even more critical issue when the state received a waiver for its workfare program, mandating the participation of all mothers with children six months old and older. In most jurisdictions where such a waiver was obtained, the state could not fully implement the program because of the shortage of day care. Detroit actually opted not to implement the state workfare program saying it was too expensive. (By contrast, Richmond exercised its option to require workfare for food stamps recipients, in addition to the mandated program for AFDC and general assistance recipients).

Particularly wide-range tightening of eligibility occurred in employment programs, although not as explicitly as in health and social service programs. Because of the focus provided by the Job Training

27. Durman, Davis, and Bovbjerg, "Block Grants and the New Federalism," p. 29.

Partnership Act on productivity and on closer involvement with private sector businesses, employment programs in all four local sites directed services toward the most trainable applicants; those groups particularly disadvantaged were long-term welfare recipients and youth. Boston's agency for jobs training raised its entrance requirements; Detroit tightened its screening process and reduced the number of training slots for youth.

Changes in Service Coverage and Quality

Not all changes in service delivery were directly tied to eligibility changes. Many states limited medicaid coverage of optional services, especially eyeglasses, prescriptions, medical devices, and laboratory services. Not only did they limit what services could be covered, but they also frequently limited who could provide the services—for example, requirements to obtain eyeglasses from a bulk provider, or to have laboratory work done at certain approved locations. Such requirements potentially limited service accessibility, since not every community had approved providers.

At the local level, cost-cutting often meant reductions in staff. Local agencies argued that caseload size could be increased and each worker could work harder to compensate for the reduced staff, allowing the agency to maintain the same range and amount of services. However, qualitative differences were evident; for example,

- Wayne County Department of Social Services made staff reductions according to seniority, thus disproportionately reducing their child protective services staff because they had recently gained new positions. The department compensated by shifting workers from other service specialities into child protective services—with the net result that less-experienced workers were doing the crisis intervention.
- In San Diego all child welfare services suffered staff reductions, especially the emergency response unit. With the resulting higher caseloads, workers reported that their response time was significantly longer and they essentially ignored all except the most dangerous situations.
- In all four sites the school districts reported staff reductions, sometimes teachers and often administrative and support service staff. A notable exception was Detroit, where the school district took advantage of a temporary state waiver to increase the size of special education classes.

Payment Changes

States and localities also reduced service accessibility and thus utilization by changing payment levels and reimbursement schedules. To control rising health care costs many states placed limits on the allowable number of hospital days and on reimbursements to private physicians. The result was that physicians became less inclined to serve medicaid clients because they could not cover their costs, or the physicians charged the clients the extra cost (states have the option of imposing copayments for optional services). Local health providers used a similar method to cope with reductions in medicaid coverage: Boston and Detroit health clinics began charging fees. Clients who could not pay were referred to outpatient departments of the public hospitals.

A similar movement toward fee-for-service has occurred in day care: as public subsidies decrease, providers need an increasing proportion of fee-paying participants in order to support the children subsidized by public funds. When Richmond lowered its child care reimbursement rate for centers to the level for family homes, bringing the rate well below operating costs, centers began actively recruiting more fee-paying families.

More extreme cost-cutting actions by states and localities included reducing AFDC and general assistance grant awards (in Michigan), freezing foster care rates for board (in Michigan), eliminating training stipends and day care services in workfare programs (in numerous states), and closing particular local service facilities or reducing hours of operation (in all four local sites). Such actions pass along the problems without offering possible solutions; they are last-resort efforts by states and localities to control rising costs in the face of falling revenues.

Concluding Comments

In all areas—social services, health, employment, education, income support—children's services have undergone significant changes at the state and local levels. The federal funding losses have generally been mitigated by increased state support, and children's services have been designated as a relatively high priority in many states. To the extent that states have been seriously constrained by the recession as well as large federal cutbacks, children (and other groups) have suffered reductions in the quantity and quality of services and have experienced limitations in geographic availability of services and cuts in benefit levels. As these difficulties magnify the needs of some population groups, the "buck is passed" to local governments and thence to local service providers, both public and private nonprofit agencies. How did these agencies cope with reduced federal *and* state and local revenues? To address this question the following chapter examines nonprofit organizations serving children and youth.

CHAPTER 4

THE RESPONSE OF THE NONPROFIT SECTOR

A key ingredient in President Reagan's domestic policy strategy has been the nonprofit sector. As government service programs have been cut back, the voluntary or charitable sector has been expected to step in to fill the gap in human services programs. Nonprofit human services organizations have long been active in areas that are also the purview of government, and have offered alternatives to or complements for publicly provided services. Nonprofit organizations themselves have been directly affected by budget cuts in two fundamental ways. First, a substantial share of their income derives from government grants; as grant awards have decreased, the revenues of these nonprofit organizations have declined. Second, demand for their services has increased in response to reduced levels of government-provided direct services and income transfers. Thus nonprofit organizations simultaneously have faced cuts in government revenues and increases in service demand. "Stepping in to fill the gap" has not been a simple matter.

The extent to which nonprofit organizations can respond to government cutbacks has depended on several factors. Most important has been their dependence on public funds: the more an agency relies on government grants and contracts to finance its service efforts, the more severe is the budget reduction it likely faces and the more difficult it is to find sufficient replacement funds. A second important factor has been the commitment of the nonprofit organization to serve the most needy of the public agencies' clients. Some service areas have been clearly government-dominated (for instance, income assistance programs), while in other areas government primarily hires private agencies by contract to provide services (such as day care). The service areas in which nonprofit organizations have been active are most likely to be ones in which they seek to take a broader role as government withdraws.

This chapter, with its focus on nonprofit agencies serving children and youth, draws on the findings of the Nonprofit Sector project currently under way at The Urban Institute. The project is a three-year effort to examine the scope and operations of the private nonprofit sector in the United States and to assess the effects of recent governmental retrenchment on nonprofit organizations and the recipients of services they provide. The project has gathered extensive data on government spending in areas of interest to nonprofit organizations and on government's use of those organizations to deliver services; it has also surveyed nonprofit organizations in twelve metropolitan areas and four rural counties to investigate the effects of recent government policy changes. These communities were carefully chosen to represent a cross-section of the nation in terms of region, size of community, economic condition, population composition, and amount of human services offered. Of the 3,411 nonprofit organizations surveyed, 32 percent were identified as primarily serving children and youth.[1]

The remainder of this chapter looks in detail at the direct effects of government cutbacks on the budgets of these nonprofit organizations and at how they have been able to recoup their losses through other funding sources. The discussion then examines the implications of budget changes on service delivery, specifically the effects on demand and on the quality and quantity of services provided.

The Funding Base

Government—whether federal, state, or local—has a major presence in the functioning of nonprofit children's agencies. In 1982 most agencies received funds from some level of government, and the average agency derived more than 40 percent of its funds from those public sources.

The primacy of government funds compared to the other revenue sources tapped by nonprofit agencies serving children is shown in table 12.[2] This pattern holds true for most types of agencies serving children, although the precise level of reliance on public funding varies by the

---

1. An organization is designated as one that primarily serves children and youth, depending on age of the recipient population, services provided, and relative amount of funds expended on services to children and youth. See the appendix for more details on the Nonprofit Sector project.

2. Many of the tables presented in this chapter utilize a subset of 750 agencies serving children that provided detailed information for fiscal years 1981 and 1982 on their total expenditures and the share of those expenditures coming from government. Only with this complete data was it possible to examine actual changes in government support between the two years.

TABLE 12

REVENUE SOURCES FOR AGENCIES SERVING CHILDREN IN FISCAL 1982

Revenue Source	Percent of Total Revenues from Each Source	Percent of Agencies with Any Support from Source
Government	42.4	59.2
Dues, fees, charges	21.5	69.9
United Way	8.3	30.4
Religious organizations	2.4	14.7
Other federated organizations	0.6	6.3
Direct contributions by individuals	7.9	58.0
Corporate gifts	3.5	32.5
Foundation grants	3.4	37.3
Endowment and investment income	5.1	31.7
Product sales and special fund-raisers	4.3	24.0

SOURCE: Based on 750 agencies included in the Nonprofit Sector project's 1982 survey of nonprofit organizations.

type of services provided. For example, institutional and residential care facilities rely on government for over 60 percent of their revenues, more than any other group of agencies serving children (see table 13). These are also the largest of the groupings of the agencies, suggesting a direct correlation between receipt of government money and agency size. These agencies tend to be group homes and children's residential facilities, probably deriving their public support from Title IV(E), which was formerly Title IV(A), and medicaid.

The hypothesis that government funds make agencies large is supported by the data for day care agencies, which show a surprisingly high aggregate reliance on government funding. The government funds flow mainly to large day care centers, often from Head Start. Of the 170 day care agencies providing complete revenue information, 78 received no support from the government but relied instead on service fees and, increasingly, on United Way and other private funding sources. Not surprisingly, almost all these agencies without government support have total revenues under $100,000. By contrast, the day care agencies with funding of more than $8 million all rely heavily on government support.

Agencies serving children that are grouped under "mixed services" similarly enjoy substantial support from public sources. These agencies focus primarily on employment counseling, training, and job development, on recruitment and training of volunteers, and on multiservices—mixes of social services, health, and other services. The most

TABLE 13

RELIANCE ON GOVERNMENT FUNDING BY AGENCIES SERVING CHILDREN
IN FISCAL 1982

Agency type	*Percent of Agency Revenues from Government*
Institutional and residential care	62.1
Day care	58.5
Mixed services[a]	52.0
Health and mental health	49.2
Social services (excluding day care)	48.0
Education and research	31.4
Recreation	9.2

SOURCE: Same as table 12.

a. Includes agencies engaged primarily in employment and training, housing and community development, legal services and advocacy, or multiservice areas.

distinguishable federal programs are those created by the Comprehensive Employment and Training Act of 1973 and the Juvenile Justice and Delinquency Prevention Act, although the agencies of concern here are generally larger than most children's agencies and probably derive their funding from a wide variety of government-supported human services programs.

Child-oriented health and mental health agencies are less dependent on government support than might be expected, given the dominance of medicaid in health services financing. The three health block grants (maternal and child health, preventive health, and mental health) appear to be as important federal sources as medicaid for these largely community-based organizations, which supplement their public funds mainly through service charges and also through investments and direct individual donations.

Social services agencies focusing on children rely nearly as much as health providers do on government support. Federal funds come largely from the social services block grants, with additional support from Title IV(B), Title IV(E), and the juvenile justice and delinquency prevention program. Some of the most frequently provided social services include individual and family counseling, information and referral, juvenile delinquency prevention services, and day care. The largest social service agency is totally dependent on government funding, while the majority of those with no government support have revenues under $100,000. Support from the private sector comes largely from service fees, and the United Way is traditionally a strong supporter of social services agencies.

Education and research organizations and recreation organizations are the children's agencies that are least dependent on government support. Education agencies largely direct their services toward special populations such as the deaf, children with cerebral palsy, or youth in correctional institutions. These agencies generally engage in other, complementary, services too; private schools per se have been excluded from the survey sample. Recreation agencies similarly offer a variety of services, primarily recreational but also arts or cultural activities; most agencies additionally offer employment and training or education services. More than half the agencies in the education and research category and a similar proportion of those in the recreation group received no public sector funding in fiscal 1982, relying instead on fees, dues, and service charges and on contributions from individuals. Recreation agencies additionally derived more than 10 percent of their revenues from United Way and from special fund-raising efforts. The federal programs serving children that were most commonly tapped were Head Start (by education and research agencies) and programs created by the Comprehensive Employment and Training Act (by recreation agencies).

As mentioned, next to government, the most important funding source for nonprofit organizations serving children is dues, fees, and charges—revenues that come from service recipients. Seventy percent of the agencies utilize this source of revenue to some extent, making it the most broadly tapped of any source. The agencies most reliant on this source specialize in recreation services or education and research.

That these two sources—government funds and dues and fees—are the largest revenue contributors and are the most broadly tapped of all the funding sources deserves special notice, for they are potentially contradictory in focus. Government funds tend to be directed toward the most needy members of society, and indeed these funds are perceived that way by nonprofit agencies. Sixty percent of nonprofit children's agencies believe that government funding has caused the nonprofit agencies to direct more services to the disadvantaged; those agencies more dependent on government support express this more strongly than others. On the other hand, the use of dues, fees, and other charges for services requires a recipient population that is able to contribute to the cost of service delivery; that population is generally not poor or otherwise disadvantaged persons. The fact that most children's agencies appear to rely on both these funding sources testifies to the diversity of focus regarding recipients they serve. Such diversity may be a key to survival: only one in two

organizations offering children's services pays even moderate attention
to the poor (that is, the poor constitute more than 10 percent of
recipients) and only 28 percent identify the poor as their major target
group (defined as constituting more than 50 percent of the agency's
recipients). By contrast, 71 percent of the children's agencies moderately target their services to the working class and 52 percent predom-
inantly do so; this population is generally in need of a wide range of
human services, and is often more able to pay for some portion of
that help than are the poor.

The remainder of funds supporting nonprofit organizations serving
children in fiscal 1982 came from numerous other sources in the private
sector. United Way contributed more than 8 percent to children's
agencies' budgets and reached almost 30 percent of the agencies; social
services agencies were the favored recipients. Direct contributions by
individuals provided nearly as much funding but were much more
prevalent than United Way support: well over half of the children's
agencies counted on income from individuals; this was especially true
of recreation organizations, including such groups as the Boys' Club
and the YMCA.

Religious organizations, another component of private sector
contributions, provided a small but understated portion of nonprofit
revenues. Churches were excluded from the survey, thus effectively
eliminating the religious donations made by individuals to their home
churches. What is included here is funds provided by churches and
other religious organizations to nonprofit children's agencies, especially
residential care facilities such as group homes, detention centers, and
the like. Fifteen percent of nonprofit children's agencies receive such
funds. Religious organizations tend to favor their affiliates: 19 percent
of nonprofit children's agencies have a formal religious affiliation,
compared to 12 percent for all nonprofit agencies.

Corporate gifts and foundation grants make up a fairly small
proportion of agency revenues but again are important complements
to other monies. Three and a half percent of children's agencies fiscal
1982 funds came from each of these sources and reached approximately
one-third of the children's agencies. Most common agencies to receive
such support were those providing recreation services. Corporations
and foundations constitute important potential sources of funds to
partially replace declining federal funding sources, but the extent to
which children's agencies already have "a foot in the door" may be
a critical factor in their ability to increase such support.

A similarly modest amount of income is derived from endowments
and from special fund-raising events. Endowment and investment

income accounts for 5 percent of fiscal 1982 revenues for children's agencies; this source was used by 30 percent of the agencies, more often the larger social services organizations and recreation organizations than the smaller and relatively new children's agencies. Sales of products and special fund-raising events accounted for more than 4 percent of children's agency revenues but was used by less than a quarter of them, most often by organizations that offer recreation and social services.

In sum, nonprofit agencies serving children derive most of their revenues from government (42 percent) and from earned income in the form of dues, fees, and service charges (22 percent). The most heavily reliant on public monies are those nonprofit organizations specializing in institutional and residential care and day care. By contrast, the heaviest users of dues and fees are recreation agencies and education and research organizations. The balance of revenues of nonprofit organizations come from a variety of sources: 8 percent each from United Way and direct individual giving; 5 percent from endowment and investment income; and less than 5 percent each from religious and other federated giving, corporations, foundations, and special fund-raising events.

The diversity of the government programs and the sources in the private sector that support nonprofit children's organizations would appear to enhance the ability of these organizations to cope with government cutbacks in funding. Whether these child-serving nonprofit organizations are able to respond depends in large part on how severely they individually are affected by the budget cuts, and on how much private funding could be obtained. The following section turns to these questions.

Changes in Government Support

Table 14 suggests the breadth of the impact of government funding changes on children's organizations. Well over a fourth of the agencies faced decreases in public dollars, and an additional 39 percent saw no change in government funding. As a result, most children's organizations were left ill-equipped to operate in the inflationary economy. Fairly few children's agencies grew substantially during this period, suggesting that the burden of meeting the increasing community needs described in the previous chapter was proving too heavy for most of the organizations that the Reagan administration believed would "fill the gap."

TABLE 14

PERCENT CHANGE IN GOVERNMENT SUPPORT
OF AGENCIES SERVING CHILDREN,
FISCAL YEARS 1981–82

Percent Change in Government Support	Percent of Children's Agencies
Substantial decrease[a]	15
Moderate decrease[b]	13
No change	39
Moderate increase[b]	22
Substantial increase[a]	10

SOURCE: Based on 744 agencies included in the Nonprofit Sector project's 1982 survey
of nonprofit organizations.
a. A change of 25 percent or more.
b. A change of less than 25 percent.

Although the aggregate picture of funding for children's agencies does not look particularly rosy, the difficulties become clearer when one differentiates among the seven types of agencies. Table 15 pinpoints the winners and the losers between fiscal years 1981 and 1982. Overall, children's organizations held their own in nominal terms but weathered a modest real decrease of 3.4 percent. This compares favorably to the 6.3 percent real decrease experienced by all the nonprofit agencies surveyed.

Among the different service areas, health-related agencies were the only ones to experience increases in government support after adjusting for inflation. Continued growth in medicaid and in state and local government support more than compensated for the losses sustained from federal block grants in health. Child-focused health and mental health agencies fared significantly better than their total survey counterparts (all health agencies included in the survey, which had a real decrease of about 1 percent), although even these growing agencies noted severe losses in particular health areas such as community health centers. Institutional and residential care facilities for children fared less well than such facilities in the total survey population (which witnessed a real increase of 4.3 percent), largely because these children's agencies tended to be group homes and residential centers that did not rely as heavily on the growing medicaid and medicare programs as did nonprofit institutions overall. Nonetheless, these residential facilities did feel the effects of government policy changes; one agency heavily dependent on public monies and facing a large decrease in those funds noted a change in service focus: "Programs

TABLE 15

Change in Government Support for Nonprofit Agencies and Nonprofit
Agencies Serving Children, by Service Focus, Fiscal Years 1981–82

| | | Percent Change in Government Revenues | |
Type of Agency and Service Focus	Number of Agencies	Nominal Change	Inflation-Adjusted Change
Nonprofit agencies	2,304	−0.7	−6.3
Nonprofit agencies serving children	750	2.3	−3.4
Service focus			
Health and mental health	42	19.1	12.4
Institutional and residential care	53	6.1	0.1
Mixed[a]	126	2.0	−3.8
Social services (excluding day care)	115	1.1	−4.6
Day care	170	−2.0	−7.5
Education and research	80	−2.4	−7.9
Recreation	157	−5.9	−11.2

Source: Based on the Nonprofit Sector project's 1982 survey of nonprofit organizations.
    a. Includes agencies engaged primarily in employment and training, housing and
community development, legal services and advocacy, or multiservice areas.

that were developed to access and reach out to at-risk populations
have had to become more institutional in approach to continue funding
. . . the population the service was designed for is almost excluded by
new criteria and requirements."[3]

All other categories of children's agencies suffered budgetary
losses in inflation-adjusted terms. The mixed category, including largely
employment and training agencies and multiservice organizations, lost
less than 4 percent of its aggregate government support, much less
than might have been expected given the magnitude of the federal cuts
to employment programs. Most of these agencies that lost large amounts
of public support did indeed lose monies appropriated by the Comprehensive Employment and Training Act, but they also relied on state
funding and, more so than their total survey counterparts, on nongovernmental funding sources.

Nonprofit agencies serving children fared better in social services,
where federal reductions exceeded 18 percent in fiscal years 1981 and
1982, than did nonprofit social services agencies in the total survey
population. Children's social services agencies (excluding day care)
registered a 5 percent real decrease, compared to 8 percent for all

3. Comment by one respondent who participated in the 1982 survey of the Nonprofit
Sector project.

social services agencies. This can be explained by several trends in public child welfare services (discussed in detail in chapter 3). First, states did not generally pass on Title XX cuts proportionately to all service areas; child welfare services were often a high priority and so were cut relatively less than other social services. Second, new federal dollars for foster care and adoption assistance began flowing to states under the Adoption Assistance and Child Welfare Act, which was passed just before legislation for the social services block grant, and thus counteracted some of the funding losses that accompanied creation of the block grant. Third and most important, public child welfare services are at least half supported by nonfederal funds; funds from the social services block grants thus have relatively less impact on children's services than on other social services. Indeed, the largest children's social services agencies among those responding to The Urban Institute survey rely on local and state support in addition to or instead of federal government funding. Their varied services tend to be designed for broad family needs, thus increasing their appeal to general fund decision-makers at the state and local levels.

Child day care agencies similarly show less decrease in government support than social services agencies in the total survey population, although their 7.5 percent inflation-adjusted loss is substantial. Small day care agencies received little if any government support, and so held steady during the 1981–82 period. The larger day care centers are generally supported by money from either the social services block grant or Head Start, or rely on a variety of federal social services programs to supplement their primary efforts in the day care area. In fiscal 1982 Head Start funding was twice that of the social services block-grant funding that went to day care. Several individual day care centers that relied heavily on these funds were devastated, but the Head Start centers remained relatively steady, making the aggregate effect on day care agencies look less severe than it was for all surveyed social services agencies.

Faring somewhat worse than day care agencies were the education and research organizations, largely educational programs for special populations. Although many of these agencies tapped federal funds appropriated by the Comprehensive Employment and Training Act, the social services block grant, and the Elementary and Secondary Education and Education Consolidation and Improvement Acts, their limited governmental support came more often from special state programs that, in times of tightening budgets, tended to be reduced or eliminated (see the discussion on education in the section entitled "Priorities among Services" in chapter 3).

Recreation-oriented agencies that serve children stand out as the only group recording double-digit reductions in government support after adjusting for inflation. These agencies suffered substantially more than all surveyed organizations specializing in recreation and in culture and arts, even though the children's recreation agencies as a rule received an even smaller share of their revenues from government (9 percent) than their total survey counterparts (14 percent). The federal government funds that these recreation agencies received were primarily funds mandated by the Comprehensive Employment and Training Act for public service employment positions and for youth training. The act was repealed by the Reagan administration, and replaced by the Job Training Partnership Act, which lacked specific funding for either public service jobs or for youth training.

In summary, agencies serving children appeared to fare better than the total survey population of nonprofit organizations, but they nonetheless experienced losses in government support in particular service areas. The *individual organizations* that fared best in the face of government policy changes were those that were either involved in delivering medicaid-related health services or were initially largely independent of government funding. In the areas of day care, recreation, and education and research, two types of agencies appeared to coexist: the larger, government-supported organizations that suffered large dollar losses and the somewhat smaller ones that were not linked to government financially. The former type dominates when measured in terms of aggregate expenditures and in terms of sheer volume of services available so that, although the existence of privately supported children's agencies is an encouraging sign, the fact remains that government cutbacks have seriously harmed the major nonprofit providers of children's social services, day care, education and research, and recreation services.

The Response: Appeal to Other Funding Sources

Despite their losses in government financial support, nonprofit children's agencies as a group were able to grow modestly between 1981 and 1982, after adjusting for inflation. Average spending for the 750 children's agencies increased by 2.1 percent in real terms, and recovery among the total survey population of nonprofit agencies was 0.5 percent. From what sources did these agencies obtain these much-needed "replacement" dollars? As Table 16 indicates, agencies turned to a variety of sources in the private sector, all of which increased their funding to nonprofit agencies between fiscal years 1981 and 1982.

TABLE 16

CHANGE IN INCOME OF THE AVERAGE AGENCY SERVING CHILDREN,
BY SOURCE OF SUPPORT, FISCAL YEARS 1981–82

Source	Income from Source (1981 Dollars) 1982	Change, 1981– 82	Percent Change, 1981–82
Government	253,223	−9,007	−3.4
United Way	49,582	1,158	2.4
Religious and other federated organizations	17,418	394	2.3
Direct contributions by individuals	47,105	3,777	8.7
Corporate gifts	20,961	1,236	6.3
Foundation grants	20,475	1,786	9.6
Dues, fees, charges	128,586	9,597	8.1
Endowment and investment income	30,667	308	1.0
Product sales and special fund-raisers	25,893	2,574	11.0
Unallocated to source	3,876	517	. . .
Total	597,786	12,340	2.1

SOURCE: Based on 750 agencies included in the Nonprofit Sector project's 1982 survey of nonprofit organizations.

The magnitude of the increases varied greatly among the funding sources, as did the real dollar value of the changes. Earned income, although not the source with the largest percentage increase, was clearly the most important replacement, bringing into the average agency more new dollars than were lost in the government cutbacks. Dues, fees, and service charges alone completely offset the aggregate losses in public support.

Beyond the new funds coming from service recipients, individual citizens showed their support of children's services by increases in several forms of private donations: United Way and religious and other federated giving, each 2 percent above 1981 levels, and direct donations by individuals, nearly 9 percent above that of 1981 and adding a noticeable $3,777 to the income stream of the typical nonprofit agency serving children. Both United Way and direct individual donations grew proportionately more in importance for agencies serving children than for the total survey sample of nonprofit organizations, which showed increases of 1.9 percent in United Way and 7.9 percent in direct contributions. This contrast suggests a shift toward supporting smaller agencies than in the past.

Children's agencies also received a significant boost from corporate and foundation sources, which increased a healthy 6 and 10 percent, respectively, beyond inflation. Agencies serving children fared much better than all surveyed nonprofit organizations, which actually experienced real declines in corporate and foundation support. Foundation and corporate gifts provided only a modest 7 percent of the average children's agency's budget in fiscal 1982, but the sudden boost nonetheless helped to compensate for government losses. The discrepancy between agencies serving children and all surveyed nonprofit agencies reflects a growing tendency to shift more resources toward smaller organizations and toward those involved in social services.

The largest percentage increase in funding for children's agencies was from product sales and special fund-raising events. This source contributed $2,574 more to the typical agency in 1982 than in 1981. Nonetheless, such income remained a small part of the average budget, moving from 4.0 percent to 4.3 percent of the average agency's 1982 budget.

The picture presented in table 16 illustrates clearly how agencies serving children compensated for their lost government revenues by turning to a variety of other funding sources. The increase in dues, fees, and charges alone replaced the government loss, and substantial real dollar gains from private contributions, corporations and foundations, and special fund-raising events brought the average children's organization $12,000 into the black. However, this aggregate view obscures significant differential effects among the individual agencies. Increased support from United Way or new corporate gifts did not necessarily go to the agencies that lost the most government funds. The 2 percent real growth in nonprofit revenues translates into *declines* in the budgets of 43 percent of children's agencies, after adjusting for inflation. Of the eighteen agencies that lost $200,000 or more in government funds, thirteen were unable to replace even half of the public monies lost due to government policy changes. Seven agencies made up none of the government losses—those specialized in social services, employment and training, and multiple services.

Table 17 presents a detailed picture of funding changes for seven different types of children's agencies, indicating the proportionate change in inflation-adjusted income flowing from each funding source to each type of service agency. Among the different service groupings, recreation agencies fared the best and recovered well from a high percentage loss in government support. These agencies relied only modestly on government; the loss of 11 percent represented less than $7,000 (in 1981 dollars), compared to the average recreation agency budget of nearly $600,000. The replacement funding came largely from dues and service fees and from special fund-raising events. In sharp

TABLE 17

Percent Change in Funding of Nonprofit Children's Agencies, by Service Focus, Fiscal Years 1981–82

Source	Recreation	Institutional and Residential Care	Health and Mental Health	Mixed Services[a]	Education and Research	Day Care	Other Social Services	All Children's Agencies
Government	-11.2	0.1	12.4	-3.8	-7.9	-7.5	-4.6	-3.4
United Way	4.5	-3.1	0.4	-1.0	-1.1	21.6	-2.3	2.4
Religious and other federated organizations	-4.6	5.4	-27.5	3.7	3.5	-7.3	3.3	2.3
Direct contributions by individuals	9.3	21.5	-10.0	17.3	-0.2	4.8	6.4	8.7
Corporate gifts	-2.7	7.6	-14.0	16.1	14.6	12.4	15.9	6.3
Foundation grants	16.7	57.0	-10.4	-1.7	7.1	-6.0	-3.6	9.6
Dues, fees, charges	10.4	13.6	4.2	15.4	3.7	7.7	-4.4	8.1
Endowment and investment	2.1	14.4	11.6	-4.4	-2.0	-7.4	-5.0	1.0
Product sales and special fund-raisers	15.9	25.9	-10.2	1.9	4.4	-6.2	10.1	11.0
Total	6.6	5.9	5.5	2.0	-1.1	-1.1	-3.0	2.1

Source: Based on 750 agencies included in the Nonprofit Sector project's 1982 survey.

a. Includes agencies engaged primarily in employment and training, housing and community development, legal services and advocacy, or multiservice areas.

contrast to all the surveyed nonprofit recreation and culture agencies, children's recreation agencies also saw significant increases in support from foundations and from direct individual donations.

Institutional and residential care facilities saw the largest dollar increase in the average agency budget. These organizations generally did not face government cuts, so their growth cannot be characterized as a recovery. Large gains were made in direct individual donations, foundation grants, service fees, and endowment income; this increased income is in sharp contrast to that of all surveyed nonprofit agencies of this type, which primarily increased government support. Institutional and residential care facilities for children showed real growth in eight out of nine funding areas; only United Way support declined, in apparent response to greater need in other service areas.

Health and mental health agencies were unique in not maintaining the funding increase that came from government. On average, these agencies brought in $32,000 more (in 1981 dollars) in government support, but lost support in other areas so that their overall revenues grew only $31,000. Health-related children's agencies lost much ground in individual donations, with smaller losses in corporate and foundation support. These private funding sources appear to have withdrawn support from the children's agencies favored by government in order to bolster the shrinking budgets of other hard-hit agencies.

Agencies providing day care faced one of the largest decreases in government funding but managed to recover through increased reliance on United Way and on service charges. A good sign of changing times came from corporations, which substantially increased their support of day care centers, although the corporate funds still were less than 1 percent of total fiscal 1982 revenues. Day care centers showed somewhat better recovery capability than all surveyed social services agencies, perhaps because of their smaller size and their greater ability to turn to service fees.

Children's social services agencies (excluding day care) demonstrated the least recovery of any group of agencies serving children, and they showed less recovery than their total survey counterparts. Total revenue losses for these agencies exceeded their dollar losses from government ($21,000 compared to $16,000). Increases in funds from corporations and from individual contributions were each about $2,000, not enough to compensate both for government losses and for inflation. In addition, funding from each of the two largest sources of private funding for children's social services, United Way and service fees, failed to keep pace with inflation between 1981 and 1982. These spelled the difference between the fate of children's social services agencies and of social services agencies in the total survey sample, for which both United Way and service fees grew by modest amounts. It seems clear that day care services were favored over other child social services for United Way increases, although on the balance United Way support to social services agencies represented a larger part of those agency budgets than the budgets of day care centers (15 percent and 12 percent, respectively, in 1982).

Education and research organizations fared much like day care centers in making up much of their lost government support, but they turned to very different sources. The biggest increases came from corporations, foundations, and especially from service charges. Religious and other federated funds also significantly increased their support in percentage terms, although the dollar contribution remained relatively small. Direct individual donations, a mainstay of education budgets, barely kept pace with inflation. This was in sharp contrast to the experience of all surveyed nonprofit education and research organizations, which showed 7 percent growth in individual contributions after adjusting for inflation.

The remainder of the agencies serving children—the employment, housing, advocacy and multiservice organizations denoted as "mixed"— adjusted remarkably well to government declines. Their replacement funds came primarily from increased service charges, direct individual donations, and corporations. The end result was 2 percent growth beyond inflation, with the majority of revenues still coming from government. These children's agencies fared much better than their national counterparts, largely because the hardest hit organizations (legal services, housing, employment) are less common among agencies serving children than in the total survey population of nonprofits.

Although in the aggregate children's organizations recovered well from government cutbacks and the effects of inflation, there are clearly many reasons for alarm. Agencies in certain service areas were unable to stimulate enough new funding to avoid serious reductions in service levels. Social services agencies, day care centers, and education and research organizations all failed to recover from significant losses in public support. Just as state and local governments proved unable to compensate for federal program reductions in these key areas, so too the nonprofit sector was unable to meet the challenge. Even with corporations shifting their focus and with direct individual donations going more frequently to the types of service agencies most hurt by government policy changes, a great many social services, day care, education and research, and other children's agencies simply could not continue to operate as they had in 1981.

The problems in agencies with net revenue losses are only the tip of the iceberg. There are, additionally, many agencies that have kept their budgets balanced only by turning increasingly to service fees and charges. Nearly one-third of the sampled agencies serving children instituted or increased service fees during 1982, leading to an 8 percent increase in the funds from that source. Although those new monies did much to substitute for lost budgetary power due to government cutbacks, the obvious costs to service recipients must not be over-looked. Many potential clients, in need of services, may be discouraged from seeking help or may even be refused service because they cannot afford to pay. This and other service-delivery problems affecting clients are the focus of the next section.

The Effects of Cutbacks on Service Delivery

While on balance funding levels appear to have been on the favorable side for most types of agencies serving children, it is important to recognize that budgets do not tell the whole story. Nonprofit agencies provide services that complement the efforts of public agencies. In times of federal retrenchment, the private sector often provides substitutes for government-provided services that are being reduced. When a public social services agency reduces benefits or curtails services, recipients may look to the job-counseling services at the YMCA or the soup kitchen run by the local church. These alternatives offered by nonprofit organizations may not fully replace the lost food stamps and employment training program, but they may be the only options available to needy individuals.

Nonprofit agencies thus feel the effects of economic recession and government policy changes not only through direct reductions in their budgets but, perhaps more dramatically, through increased demand for their services, often from segments of the population that they have not regularly served in the past. This growing demand for services is a rough measure of growing needs in the population.

Changes in Demand

Table 18 indicates the nature of changes in service demand experienced by children's agencies between 1981 and 1982. Because it is difficult to distinguish an ordinary pattern of change from one due to particular government actions, the table examines demand changes

TABLE 18

CHANGE IN DEMAND FOR SERVICES PROVIDED BY NONPROFIT AGENCIES AND
NONPROFIT CHILDREN'S AGENCIES, BY SERVICE FOCUS, FISCAL YEARS 1981–82

Type of Agency and Service Focus		Percent of Agencies with Change in Funding Specified		
	Number	Increase	No Change	Decrease
Nonprofit Agencies	2,936	44.0	49.0	8.0
Agencies serving children	967	40.0	51.0	10.0
Service focus				
Mixed services[a]	170	61.2	32.9	5.9
Social services (excluding day care)	158	54.4	38.6	7.0
Health and mental health	64	53.1	43.8	3.1
Education and research	105	34.3	60.0	5.7
Recreation	171	30.4	62.6	7.0
Institutional and residential	66	28.8	47.0	24.2
Day care	233	22.7	62.2	15.0

SOURCE: Based on Nonprofit Sector project's 1982 survey of nonprofit organizations.
  a. Includes agencies engaged primarily in employment and training, housing and community development, legal services and advocacy, or multiservice areas.

among these agencies serving children compared to changes experienced by all surveyed nonprofit organizations.

Nonprofit children's agencies most often experienced stable demand for their services, although a substantial number of them saw rising demand. Increases were noted less often by children's organizations than by nonprofit organizations overall (40 percent versus 44 percent), primarily because of the differing service orientation of the two groups. Largely excluded from the agencies serving children are legal services and employment training programs, those hardest hit by government cutbacks and thus the areas that experienced the largest rise in service demand.

A closer look at demand changes among children's agencies with various service focuses reveals again the diversity among these agencies. It is not surprising to see that social services agencies (excluding day care centers) and mixed agencies (employment, advocacy, and so on) experienced the greatest increases in demand. These agencies registered noticeable decreases in inflation-adjusted government funding at the same time that federal support for comparable public service programs was reduced. Hence these children's services are doubly affected by government retrenchment.

By contrast, day care agencies were the least likely group to face greater demand for services and were most likely to see no change. The explanation lies in the composition of these day care agencies.

The majority are small and largely independent of government funding; they are supported by service fees and by contributions from United Way and other private sources. As small privately supported day care centers, they attract a substantially different population than the centers subsidized by the social services block grant. It is important also to remember that although day care centers as a whole faced an inflation-adjusted decrease in government support, that figure primarily reflects the situation of the minority of day care agencies—the ones that are large and federally supported.

Institutional and residential care facilities experienced the largest (although still modest) decrease in demand, perhaps partially due to the impact of the Adoption Assistance and Child Welfare Act of 1980. This act created financial incentives for public child welfare agencies to reduce their use of out-of-home care in favor of increased preventive and supportive services in order to avoid unnecessary separation of children and their families. The small group of institutional and residential care facilities sampled here includes many group homes and emergency shelter facilities.

Organizational Changes

Even among agencies that managed to replace lost government support, the shift to reliance on other funding sources often brought its own pressures for internal change. Three types of changes are discussed here, with their impact on service recipients in mind—changes in staffing, management, and service delivery.

Changes in Staffing

More than half of all children's agencies made some change in their staffing (see table 19). The organizations most likely to make staffing changes were those engaged in employment, housing, and advocacy programs (77 percent); those least likely were the education and research organizations (42 percent).

The most common type of staff change was to increase caseloads; this was done directly (29 percent of agencies), indirectly by not filling staff vacancies (21 percent of agencies), or both. Institutional and residential care facilities did not fill vacated staff positions (37 percent of agencies), perhaps in expectation of reduced caseloads due to the Adoption Assistance and Child Welfare Act of 1980. Indeed, these agencies were among the least likely to indicate they increased staff workloads (31 percent).

TABLE 19

CHANGE IN STAFFING MADE BY CHILDREN'S AGENCIES, FISCAL YEARS 1981–82

Type of Change	Number of Agencies	Percent of Agencies
Increased staff workload or caseload	312	29.4
Staff vacancies unfilled	226	21.3
Reduced administrative or support staff	210	19.8
Reduced service delivery staff	197	18.6
Salary freeze	137	12.9
Reduced staff training	120	11.3
Reduced staff benefits	85	8.0
Reduced work week for paid staff	79	7.5
None of the above	498	47.0

SOURCE: Based on 1,060 agencies included in the Nonprofit Sector project's 1982 survey of nonprofit organizations.

Reducing administrative, support, or service delivery staff were strategies selected by nearly one in every five children's organizations. Those agencies most dependent on government support—institutional and residential care facilities, employment, housing, and advocacy programs—were most likely to make these reductions. Of the latter group, 33 percent reduced support staff and 29 percent cut service staff. Employment, housing, and advocacy agencies similarly showed greater than average tendency to increase caseloads (40 percent), freeze salaries (19 percent), and reduce staff training (14 percent). The extensive changes made by this group of organizations suggests that the moderate losses in government support were probably widely spread, and that the agencies clearly anticipate further losses in the immediate future.

By contrast, social services agencies behaved much like the average children's agency, despite being among the groups hardest hit by government reductions. In only one area did they exceed all other types of children's agencies: 10 percent of the social services organizations (including day care centers) reduced the work week for paid staff. This probably translated into reduced service hours, a particularly difficult burden for users of day care centers.

Management Changes

The second type of austerity measure employed by agencies serving children was changes in management (see table 20). More children's organizations made management adjustments than made

TABLE 20

MANAGEMENT CHANGES MADE BY CHILDREN'S AGENCIES, FISCAL YEARS 1981–82

Type of Change	*Number of Agencies*	*Percent of Agencies*
Greater reliance placed on volunteers	332	31.7
Reorganized executive or administrative staff	268	25.6
New management programs to increase efficiency	262	25.0
Shared resources with other agencies	201	19.2
Joint purchase or lease of equipment or services with other agencies	64	6.1
Merged with another organization	18	1.7
None of the above	414	39.5

SOURCE: Based on 1,047 agencies included in the Nonprofit sector project's 1982 survey of nonprofit organizations.

either staffing or service delivery changes, underlining the importance that service providers give to management efficiency. Indeed, one in every four children's agencies began new management programs explicitly geared to increase efficiency.

The most frequently adopted management change was to increase reliance on volunteers; whether that means using a greater number of volunteers or using existing volunteers for a wider variety of tasks is unclear. Children's agencies have serious reservations about expanding the use of volunteers as substitutes for professionals in service delivery. But when resources shrink, the only alternative to providing services through volunteers may be to eliminate the service. The message here may be that volunteers are an increasingly vital resource as budgets get tighter and demands increase and that volunteers can assist in a variety of tasks. Currently, children's agencies use volunteers primarily to provide services directly to clients (63 percent of agencies do so). As funding constraints make reductions in support staff more necessary, volunteers may take a more active part in accounting and clerical work (currently 48 percent of agencies use volunteers in this capacity). Such a shift may have already begun: over 25 percent of agencies have reorganized their executive and administrative staff, perhaps to include more volunteers.

In addition to directly increasing management efficiency within a single organization, children's agencies have begun to explore the possibility of sharing resources with other similar organizations. Nearly one agency in five reported sharing resources. More progressive examples of this strategy include joint purchase or lease of equipment

TABLE 21

CHANGE IN SERVICE DELIVERY MADE BY CHILDREN'S AGENCIES,
FISCAL YEARS 1981–82

Type of Change	Number of Agencies	Percent of Agencies
Fees for services increased or instituted	343	32.6
Specific services or programs eliminated	172	16.3
Reduced number of clients served	135	12.8
Reduced level of service provided to individual clients	103	9.8
Tightened eligibility requirements for services	100	9.5
None of the above	514	48.8

SOURCE: Based on 1,053 agencies included in the Nonprofit Sector project's 1982 survey of nonprofit organizations.

or services (by 6 percent of children's agencies) and, at the extreme, merge with another organization. Eighteen agencies have merged, five of them engaged in social services.

Among the types of children's agencies most likely to make management changes are recreation agencies, 68 percent of which made some management adjustments. These agencies were particularly likely to increase reliance on volunteers (38 percent) because volunteer activity is particularly well suited to sports, youth clubs, and camps provided by recreation organizations. These organizations are also most likely to institute joint purchase or lease of equipment (8 percent), perhaps a van or bus to reduce transportation costs for sports teams and campers.

Service Delivery Changes

Despite extensive changes in staffing and in management practices, many nonprofit agencies serving children were nonetheless forced to make changes in service delivery. Table 21 indicates that more than half of all agencies have made some change, many of them making more than one of the listed changes. The most common behavior was to institute or increase service fees, making such earned income not only a larger (as described above) but also a more prevalent source of revenues in 1982 than it was in 1981. The social services agencies and the health and mental health organizations were most likely to choose this mechanism (36 percent and 37 percent, respectively), while institutional and residential care facilities were the least likely to turn to new or higher service charges (21 percent). The apparent inconsistency between these figures and those in table 17 can be easily explained: a few large personal care facilities increased fees while many smaller ones did not, making total revenues increase substantially, although most agencies made no such change. Institutional and residential care facilities are generally larger and less numerous than health or social services agencies, so a few large agencies have more influence on aggregate figures.

Specific services or programs were eliminated by 16 percent of children's agencies. This action was taken most frequently by children's agencies (31 percent) that tend to offer mixed employment and advocacy services, which were most drastically affected by federal policy changes.

The agencies that suffered the most severe government cutbacks were of course the most likely to make some kind of service delivery change. Six out of ten social services and mixed service agencies altered their service delivery strategies in some way, compared to half of all children's agencies. These particular organizations chose to reduce service levels or to reduce numbers of clients more often than did other types of agencies. The preliminary pattern of curtailing nonprofit service offerings in the same areas in which public services were reduced brought considerable hardship for clients. Although nearly half of the nonprofit children's agencies did *not* take any of these actions to reduce service delivery, they alone were clearly unable to meet the needs of all the clients suffering from cutbacks in public service.

Even when government dollars increased, changes were necessary. Health and mental health agencies seemed to favor tightening eligibility requirements for clients; 16 percent of the agencies did so, compared to only 10 percent of children's agencies overall. This probably came in direct response to changing federal regulations governing medicaid coverage. Again, many nonprofit agencies appeared unable to shield service recipients from the hard realities of government retrenchment.

The Changing Structure of the Sector

What do these above-mentioned organizational changes and funding shifts mean in terms of the availability of needed services from the nonprofit sector? As government becomes a smaller part of the funding picture, the service priorities of private funders increasingly determine

TABLE 22

CHANGE IN SHARES OF TOTAL INCOME FLOWING TO NONPROFIT CHILDREN'S
AGENCIES, BY SERVICE FOCUS, FISCAL YEARS 1981–82

(Percent)

	Share of All Income		Percent Change in Share
Service Focus	*1981*	*1982*	
Social services			
(excluding day care)	18.6	17.7	−5.0
Day care	8.5	8.2	−3.1
Education and research	9.7	9.4	−3.1
Mixed services[a]	25.8	25.7	−0.1
Health and mental health	5.3	5.5	3.4
Institutional and residential	12.7	13.2	3.7
Recreation	19.5	20.3	4.4

SOURCE: Based on 743 agencies included in the Nonprofit Sector project's 1982 survey
of nonprofit organizations. Figures are rounded.
   a. Includes agencies primarily engaged in employment and training, housing and
community development, legal services and advocacy, or multiservice areas.

the nature of the services provided by nonprofit children's organizations. Change is already evident in the relative shares of total children's agency resources going to particular service areas. Table 22 compares the income flowing to children's organizations for each service area for 1981 and 1982. Social services, day care, and education and research organizations lost the most ground, despite the significant recovery that the last two demonstrated in finding private dollars to replace some of the lost public ones. By contrast, health and mental health agencies, institutional and residential care facilities, and recreation organizations increased their shares of children's funds.

The pattern of change is best explained by the nature of the agencies' dependence on government funds. Federal support of children's health programs grew between 1981 and 1982, in contrast to most other service areas; consequently, children's agencies specializing in health and mental health began to command a larger share of the total revenues of children's agencies. Institutional and residential care facilities also became a larger factor in the sector because they were highly dependent on government support and were able to increase those funds sufficiently to meet inflation. Recreation agencies, on the other hand, grew in sectoral importance precisely because they did not rely on public support; a cut of 11 percent in a funding source that contributed only a tenth of their budget was not devastating. More important, recreation agencies were more accustomed than other children's agencies to soliciting support from a variety of private sources; United Way grants, individual donations, service fees, and special fund-raising events remained larger parts of recreation agency budgets than they were in budgets of other children's organizations.

The losses experienced by day care, other social services, and education and research agencies can be explained by the same phenomenon of government dependence. All look to government for substantial portions of their revenues, and all received significant reductions in support between 1981 and 1982. As was noted above, social services agencies (other than day care centers) found it difficult to produce replacement funding; hence these agencies show the largest decline in their share of sector resources.

The shift toward health and recreation services and away from social and education services sounds a warning note concerning the future of children's services. Social services have long been the most income-dependent services, often designed to alleviate family stresses arising from unemployment, single parenthood, and other factors leading to low income. As government support for such programs decreases without concommitant increases in funding from the private sector, it is the poor and needy children who will suffer the most. Agencies cannot ask recipients to pay for protective services, since referrals for such help rarely come from the needy individuals; similarly, day care centers can only increase fees a certain amount before they make their service too expensive for the families that most need their help. If these and other services are to continue to be offered to the children and families who need them, funding sources in the private sector must shift their funding priorities even more than they already have. The question becomes, as government withdraws, who will be responsible for determining the appropriate allocation of resources among competing needs? This is a growing challenge to the nonprofit sector.

CHAPTER 5

OUTCOMES FOR CHILDREN
AND FAMILIES

State and local governments were able to mitigate some, but far from all, federal funding cuts imposed on human services programs in the early years of the Reagan administration. In large measure, they simply tightened their belts and passed the reductions through to their service providers, often nonprofit agencies, and to service recipients, the children and their families. Nonprofit organizations serving children were somewhat successful in replacing lost government support, especially in the areas of health and recreation, but children's social services, day care, employment, housing, and legal services organizations were unable to maintain previous service levels.

As responsibility was passed down the ladder from federal to state to local government, to nonprofit service providers, and finally to service recipients, the available coping strategies steadily decreased, as did discretionary resources. Children—or, more correctly, their parents, guardians, and other individuals responsible for their welfare—are seriously limited in the ways they have to cope with reductions in services. Adult decision makers commonly adopt three major patterns of behavior on behalf of children. First, because fewer services are available at a price families can afford (that is, services that are subsidized), parents defer routine care or settle for lower quality care. Second, because many families have lost in-kind benefits and support services, they turn more frequently to "last resort" programs such as the special supplemental food program for women, infants, and children, general assistance programs, or hospital outpatient departments. Third, because families defer routine care and utilize services less suited to their needs, their children increasingly face crises in which outside help is immediately needed.

To provide a context for understanding the varying stresses faced by families, table 23 looks at three major entitlement programs affecting children in four communities. Data are presented for aid to families with dependent children (AFDC), food stamps, and medicaid. Even

TABLE 23

CASELOAD CHANGES OF MAJOR ENTITLEMENT PROGRAMS IN FOUR COMMUNITIES,
1981–83

Program, Caseload, and Change	Boston, Massachusetts	Wayne County, Michigan	Richmond, Virginia	San Diego County, California[a]
AFDC				
Average monthly caseload (number of cases)	26,089	100,035	7,056	33,838
Percent change				
1981–82	−12	−1	0	1
1982–83	−14	5	2	1
Food stamps				
Average monthly caseload	51,533	142,369	16,902	11,701
Percent change				
1981–82	8	−5	−4	−35
1982–83	−4	14	2	−2
Medicaid				
Average monthly caseload	77,650	204,500	6,820	27,055
Percent change				
1981–82	−7	−14	−4	1
1982–83	−11	3	−6	15

SOURCE: Data provided by local officials in the four communities to The Urban Institute staff conducting the Community Impact Study (see the appendix).

a. Changes for 1982–83 are based on proposed budget levels for California's fiscal 1983 spending.

among the four communities there is evidence of substantial variation in the rates of change between 1981 and 1983. Wayne County (Detroit) suffered the largest caseload reductions in 1982; Boston, the largest in 1983. Richmond appears to have fared the best of the four, reflecting the relatively strong Virginia economy. In each year examined the participation in at least one of the entitlement programs decreased in one or more of the communities, with medicaid recipients showing the most frequent declines.

The figures in table 23 only begin to suggest the impact of government policy changes on vulnerable children and families. Hidden by the statistics are families who are counted in all the columns, who lost AFDC eligibility, medicaid eligibility and food stamp benefits. Also disguised are the number of families who received reduced levels of benefits without losing eligibility. In addition, families faced reductions in the whole range of grant programs discussed in the preceding sections, services that supplement the income and in-kind assistance from the entitlement programs.

Deferring Routine Care

As services become more expensive or less accessible, many children and families may defer seeking help with their problems. This applies especially to routine care, such as health maintenance visits, and to services with a long-term payoff, such as employment training. From the perspective of assessing nationwide or even community-wide impact of federal policy changes, such deferral behavior is particularly problematic because it cannot be easily measured. Caseload and utilization figures do not capture the amount of unmet or indirectly expressed need. Indeed, figures may show declining demand for services for which need is in fact rising. This is particularly true concerning changes in the medicaid program. Families who lose medicaid eligibility, often at the same time that they lose their AFDC benefits, find themselves without any health care insurance; in states that have programs for the medically needy, these families are forced to "spend down" their excess income before they are covered by the program.

Anecdotal evidence from four communities suggests that deferral of routine medical care has become a prevalent response to health services restrictions mandated by the Omnibus Budget Reconciliation Act. As community health clinics close or reduce their hours, restrict their service offerings, or limit services to non-medicaid or nonpaying clients, many families put off the routine, preventive health care visits, including numerous services critical to child health: prenatal care, well-baby checkups, immunizations, early and periodic screening, diagnosis, and treatment and other health testing. For example,

- When three local health centers were closed in Detroit, clients were left to find their own substitute health care. Other clinics were farther away, and transportation was often a problem. A Wayne County health department staff person summed it up: "Six hundred pregnant women and 11,000 children were left to seek services elsewhere in the community. The Sisters of Mercy opened a private center, the Urban Health Center, to pick up some of the pediatric cases and, gradually, the maternity care too. But it wasn't nearly enough."[1]
- In Richmond, limits on medicaid coverage and on transportation vouchers and reduced clinic hours have caused many families to defer early and periodic screening, diagnosis, and treatment:

1. Telephone interview with the Wayne County Health Department staff, June 1983.

"The health department only has appointments one day per week for an hour and a half, so appointments are months away for many clients. They forget or just give up."[2]

• When the San Diego County Health Department discontinued the child health and disability prevention clinics, it projected "25 percent of [affected low-income] children will go to CHDP elsewhere (out of county); 75 percent will not be eligible for other services, but most likely to be picked up by community clinics; about 1,050 infants and children under 3 will lose all services but immunizations."[3] But citizen pressure led the board of supervisors to reinstate the project; the costs were absorbed by some other county services.

A similar pattern of deferring necessary care or settling for lower quality care is found in employment-related day care services. Reductions in the availability of Title XX-supported day care and massive shifts to the Title IV(A) child care disregard provisions have generally caused working parents to use the least expensive care available. With the demise of the federal interagency day care requirements and the increasing use of the income disregard, public agencies believe they have little control over the quality of care. The Wayne County day care staff was particularly concerned: "Under Title IVA funding, we have no control over the care setting; it's not screened or regulated: a growing number of homes are taking care of the kids [rather than centers]. More and more children are exposed to unnecessary risk; no one checks the furnace, immunizations, risk of sexual abuse."[4] The staff acknowledges that these are its fears, and bemoans the lack of studies to determine if these problems are widespread.

A representative of a Boston day care consortium describes the problem from the perspective of the working mothers: "Low-income people who lose their subsidized care turn to cheaper, inadequate care, or use children as sitters, or have latch-key children." Further, "Workfare has incredible ramifications, it's very demeaning. A mother has to choose between no job and welfare so she can be at home with her child, or a job and inadequate child care."[5] The staff of the

---

2. Interview with the Richmond Department of Social Services staff, May 1983.

3. County of San Diego, *Proposed Program Budget 1982–1983*, vol. 1: *Fiscal, Public Protection, Health, Social Services* (County of San Diego, n.d.).

4. Telephone interview with the Wayne County Department of Social Services staff, June 1983.

5. Telephone interview with a representative of the Boston Area Committee on Day Care, August 1983.

Richmond Department of Social Services echoes this view of the adverse effects on work incentives: the complexity of the day care arrangements, coupled with reduced transportation vouchers to cover travel to and from day care, causes many clients to drop out of training programs.[6]

Turning to Programs of "Last Resort"

Not all service needs can be deferred. Basic necessities, such as food and shelter, simply cannot be denied to needy families. A mother may skip her infant's well-baby visits, but she needs help when the baby becomes ill; she may give up on a training program because of day care problems, but she needs income from some source. As medicaid, AFDC, food stamps and other benefits become more scarce, needy families are turning increasingly to sources of help that are not federally supported, which are often less systematic: hospital outpatient and emergency room services for nonemergency health care, locally funded general assistance or general relief programs for income support, and the WIC program for women, infants, and children and soup kitchens for food. Again the standard statistics hide the true extent of the problem: figures on emergency room utilization often do not distinguish between actual emergencies and minor ailments that can be routinely treated; soup kitchens do not ask their patrons whether or not they just lost their food stamps or AFDC benefits. The costs that are not borne by the federal entitlement programs are largely shifted to other service programs, programs in which the services might be less appropriate to the need and the cost per recipient might be higher than in the restricted program.

Neighborhood health clinics, the primary source of health care for poor families and children, have been hit twice—by reductions in maternal and child health funds from federal and state sources and by restrictions in medicaid coverage, especially for prescriptions, laboratory work, and reimbursement rates for individual physicians. Clinics are thus caught by declining state and federal grants and shrinking reimbursement; consequently, they often curtail service offerings, lower the quality of services, or refer nonpaying clients to other health care providers. For example,

- Richmond maternal and child health clinics and community health clinics use an informal quota system, referring non-

---

6. Interviews with the Richmond Department of Social Services staff, May 1983.

medicaid low-income patients to the outpatient departments of local hospitals.

• Boston's neighborhood health centers can no longer handle the increasing number of requests for free care. One center reported that 25 percent of its patients cannot pay and do not have third-party coverage. At City Hospital, 60 percent of the outpatient care and 40 percent of inpatient care is provided without reimbursement. One health center director states: "Federal actions have generally meant tighter funds for neighborhood health centers and thus consumers have to pay more. The problem with the health center movement is that it does not have ways to recover funds the way hospitals do. Some centers have raised fees, causing people to go to emergency rooms for routine care."[7]

Hospitals are also feeling the squeeze due to federal changes in both medicaid and medicare. The latter indirectly affect children insofar as the medicare constraints have caused hospitals to reduce overall services to poor families. Hospitals were in the past able to supplement funds to serve the uninsured through medicare payments, but new restrictions on the federal entitlement make it more costly for hospitals to subsidize the poor, so they often reduce their efforts. In Massachusetts the state government entered the picture: state law now requires that public hospitals serve primarily fee-paying or insured patients; clients who cannot pay and are without third-party coverage are limited to a certain percentage of the patient population. This further decreases hospital services to the uninsured poor.

Just as the federal cutbacks in medicaid, maternal and child health, and preventive health services have made proper health care less available to poor families, so too reductions in food stamps and child nutrition programs have made it harder for families to adequately feed their children. All four local communities included in the study report increasing demand for WIC services for women, infants, and children, generally considered to be the "food program of last resort" and the only federal nutrition program that was not cut. Local WIC programs have been unable to meet the rising demand for services; waiting lists are long, even where eligibility has been tightened. The Boston health department staff notes that its facilities are at capacity: the number of interview rooms and staff members are insufficient to interview new

7. Telephone interview with the director of the Boston neighborhood health center, August 1983.

applicants. In San Diego the applicant pool is becoming noticeably broader despite tighter eligibility rules—former food stamp recipients mistakenly believe the WIC program can be a general replacement for food stamps, and they are angered and discouraged by the focus on pregnant women and young children. Even among the growing group of eligibles, the services provided by WIC programs are far from meeting the need. National data on WIC eligibility and participation levels indicate that only 20 percent of all eligible women and children under age five were served in 1980; in twenty-two states the WIC programs served less than a quarter of the eligibles.[8]

Changes in the AFDC program similarly push poor families to apply for general assistance or general relief, the locally funded income support programs for people ineligible for any federally supported income-maintenance programs. General assistance typically is given to single adults; one indication of the extent to which it is being used by families that formerly were covered by AFDC is the number of families with children receiving general assistance:

- In Wayne County the caseload for general assistance increased fairly steadily each year between 1979 and 1983, due largely to high unemployment rates. However, between 1980 and 1983 the rates of increase for general assistance recipients with children were greater than the rates for general assistance overall. Between July 1981 and July 1982 the caseload of the former group grew 6 percent while the AFDC caseload declined 1 percent.
- In Boston the general relief caseload increased 14 percent between state fiscal years 1982 and 1983; the AFDC caseload fell 14 percent. There was a reportedly higher proportion of families with children among the general relief recipients.

Growing Needs in Times of Crisis

As poor children and their families defer routine preventive health care and seek basic necessities from programs and agencies not best designed to serve them, their problems often go untended, and the situation may worsen to a critical level. It is impossible to separate the effects of cutbacks in human services in the Reagan administration

---

8. Select Panel for the Promotion of Child Health, *Better Health for Our Children: A National Strategy*, vol. 3: *A Statistical Profile* (Washington, D.C.: Department of Health and Human Services, Public Health Service, 1981).

from the impact of the recession or from the fiscal difficulties of particular states; all interact to create an often untenable situation for the poor. The stress level is apparent in the growing number of reports of child abuse and neglect, higher utilization of hospital emergency rooms, and increasing incidence of malnutrition.

All four communities studied here reported increasing numbers of referrals to child protective services, suggesting increasing incidence of child abuse and neglect. Because staffing levels have not been able to keep pace with the rising caseload levels, each case reportedly receives less thorough attention. This shortage of staff time is aggravated by the fact that cases are entering the system in which families have more serious problems and more intensive service needs. The statistics on substantiated cases of child abuse and neglect may or may not reveal this trend, say protective services workers, because staffs are overloaded. In Wayne County the protective services investigations have increased every year since 1980, but substantiations have been decreasing since 1981; as a percent of investigations, substantiations have dropped from 86 percent in 1980 to 83 percent in 1981 to 67 percent in 1982. The staff believes the figures illustrate how workers deal with overload—by more tightly screening what is considered substantiation in order to keep workloads to a manageable level.[9]

All four sites similarly report higher utilization of hospital emergency rooms, often for emergency needs but also frequently for less critical needs; once a child arrives with an emergency, more serious problems become apparent. For example, a Boston survey of infants brought to City Hospital's emergency room found 15 percent of them to be below the third percentile on height or weight, the definition of malnutrition. A comparable statewide study of health centers and hospitals found 10 percent of children aged six months to six years were malnourished.[10] Boston findings are particularly disturbing in view of the state policy of explicitly targeting WIC services on children under one year of age rather than children age four and under.

The reduction in the availability of preventive health care, and in families' utilization of it, may directly lead to more serious health problems. The relation between prenatal care and infant health status at birth has been well documented. The San Diego County budget, for example, is explicit about the general effects of decreased funding for

9. Telephone interview with the Michigan Department of Social Services staff, June 1983.

10. Telephone interview with a physician at Boston City Hospital, August 1983.

primary care services: "It will create a major hardship on the poor by further reducing their already limited access to medical care. The effect will be declining health status, increased mortality from preventable causes, increased utilization of hospital care, and an adverse impact on public health."[11]

The Boston Health Department staff report overutilization of hospital inpatient facilities due to reductions in the lead-based paint poisoning program, now part of the maternal and child health block grant. An administrator of a neighborhood health center states: "Housing is our biggest problem. The lead-based paint program was cut back so there are few lead inspectors and almost no subsidies for deleading buildings. Landlords [who are often poor and rent out floors of their own homes to other families] cannot afford to delead, and the poor tenants cannot pay the hospital bills for treating the affected children. The result is that people are abandoning the houses—making the rat control problem worse."[12] And hospitals are keeping children longer than necessary because there is no safe home for them to go to— Boston City Hospital reports that 85 percent of the hospital days for "lead-poisoned children" are medically unnecessary, up from 55 percent a few years ago.[13]

Just as the reduction in available preventive health and social services has led to more crisis needs among poor families, so too the reductions in food programs have aggravated the problems of hunger and malnutrition. The Boston and Massachusetts surveys and the data comparing WIC participation and eligibility levels reveal that current funding for food stamp, WIC, and child nutrition programs (such as school lunches) is far from adequate. The U.S. Conference of Mayors prepared a report in June 1983 on hunger in American cities; all eight cities studied experienced "a recent and significant increase in the demand for emergency food assistance."[14] The report cites as causes unemployment, cutbacks in federal funding to nutrition programs, and inflation in the costs of necessities. Five of the eight cities report that they are unable to serve all those in need of food assistance, and two other cities say their resources are already at the straining point.

---

11. County of San Diego, *Proposed Program Budget 1982–1983*, vol. 1.

12. Telephone interview with a physician of a Boston neighborhood health center, August 1983.

13. Telephone interview with a physician of Boston City Hospital, August 1983.

14. U.S. Congress, Committee on Education and Labor, Subcommittee on Elementary, Secondary, and Vocational Education, *Oversight Hearing on Restoring Funding to the Child Nutrition Programs,* "Hunger in American Cities," Report of the U.S. Conference of Mayors, 98th Cong. 1 sess. (Washington, D.C.: U.S. Government Printing Office, 1984).

Concluding Comments

These cycles of behavior—deferring needed care, turning to inadequate alternatives, reaching crises—are not reducible to simple statistics. Increases in demand for last-resort programs and for crisis services *suggest* the extent of the problems. The magnitude of the federal cutbacks, plus the additional losses in particular service areas at the state and local levels, make it highly likely that many, many children are affected in the ways described above. The loss of AFDC benefits alone can trigger a whole sequence of losses, because AFDC eligibility is the criteria for entry into many support programs— medicaid, Title IV(A) child care, many training programs. Other services in short supply are increasingly using income level to select recipients—many social services, health services, nutrition programs.

It is clear that there is no one cause, nor can any one program be the solution, to the dangerous cycles of behavior followed by poor families. The systematic reductions in a broad range of programs affecting children has pushed any remedy of the problems beyond the capability of state and local governments and the nonprofit sector. What is needed is a coordinated effort by all levels of government, together with the private sector, to alleviate the basic economic and social problems that appear to be increasing their hold on children and their families, especially those with low income.

CHAPTER 6

CONCLUSIONS

The President's economic recovery program and the Omnibus Budget Reconciliation Act have had widespread impact on services to children. At the federal level, funding for programs benefiting children has been severely reduced since 1981, especially in the areas of social services and child care, nutrition, employment, education, income maintenance, and, to a lesser extent, health. At the state and local levels, governments have taken a variety of steps to respond to this drop in funding, with modest success in some service areas. By and large, however, their efforts to replace lost federal funds, give higher priorities to children's services, and engage in efficiency measures have not been sufficient to compensate for federal policy changes, particularly changes in eligibility and benefit levels for entitlement programs. At nongovernmental levels, despite the Reagan administration's assertions that the private sector has the capacity to step in to fill the gap where government has withdrawn, evidence shows that nonprofit organizations have been unable to mitigate much of the negative effect of public sector retrenchment because of their own losses in government funding. At the same time, nonprofit organizations experienced increases in the demand for their services. The revenues of these nonprofit agencies have been sustained largely through increased service fees—an unfortunate consequence of federal cutbacks because increased fees potentially exclude the most needy children and families.

Each area of children's services has suffered in a somewhat unique way through the interplay of decisions made by federal policymakers, state and local government agencies, and nonprofit organizations. The agencies that suffered least (but suffered nonetheless) specialized in health-related services; those experiencing the most severe effects were agencies providing social services. In between these two extremes in the range of agencies is a variety of other service providers that offer the needy such assistance as recreation, education, employment, and broad mixes of human services.

How the Specific Programs Fared

The following programs experienced problems as a result of federal cutbacks.

Health Services

Agencies delivering health or mental health services, including clinics as well as institutional and residential care facilities, generally had modest losses in government support, although particular services were hurt by the consolidation of categorical programs into block grants. The aggregate level of government funding remained fairly steady due to medicaid spending, which dwarfs all other outlays for health services. The most serious hardships for children were introduced in the health area because of federal changes in medicaid coverage. State and local governments revealed clear preferences for basic services over specialized or innovative ones in their use of health block grants, and for services with broader constituencies over more narrow ones. Child health services were not clearly preferred over other health services, although in most areas maternal and infant care was a high priority. Among nonprofit providers, government support actually grew between 1981 and 1982. These agencies nonetheless felt the impact of government policy changes on increased demand for their services. Overall, child health programs have balanced fairly steady funding and increased demand by limiting service offerings to basic health needs and by restricting utilization through changes in eligibility criteria, service delivery locations, or service charges.

Social Services

Agencies providing social services were drastically affected by federal cutbacks, especially in the social services block grant and Title XX programs. State governments, which generally give child welfare services high priority, made widespread efforts to replace lost federal funds and to shift resources toward children's programs, with mixed results. Crisis-oriented services were maintained, but often at the expense of preventive and supportive services. Worst hit were day care services, especially for the working poor. Support from the private sector helped but was not sufficient to compensate for losses in government funding and greatly increased demand. Nonprofit social service providers and day care agencies were forced to make significant changes, including greater reliance on service fees, reducing service levels, and restricting the numbers of persons served. Overall, despite state and local government efforts to protect children's social services, prevention services were seriously diminished, and increased service charges excluded many of the most needy families from important supportive services.

Recreation

Agencies specializing in recreation, cultural, and arts activities were relatively untouched by government retrenchment, although their modest federal support (largely from the Comprehensive Employment and Training Act) decreased significantly between 1981 and 1982. Accustomed to tapping the private sector for support, these nonprofit agencies more than recovered from their government losses through increased individual donations, support from foundations, and earned income from service charges and fees. Greater use of volunteers also enabled them to meet modest increases in service demand.

Education

Federal education assistance decreased between 1981 and 1982. Few states or local governments sought to replace the diminished federal support, leaving school districts to reduce services and staffing. The involvement of the private sector in education, excluding private schools, was limited to specialized populations and was relatively independent of government funding. The few public dollars available for education did decrease sharply but were replaced, for the most part, by corporate and foundation grants and by increased service charges.

Employment and Other Services

Youth employment programs were the services most severely curtailed by federal policy changes. State and local governments were largely unable to mitigate these losses; children and families not eligible for AFDC suffered the most. Nonprofit providers of employment training services and a mixture of other related services—some housing, advocacy, and supportive social services—were able to recover a substantial part of their government losses through increases in corporate support and in individual donations; the biggest source, however, was service fees and charges. These agencies faced the most increase in demand of any group of nonprofit children's agencies; like social services agencies they were forced to make widespread reductions in service offerings, in levels of service, and in numbers of persons served. Coming together with increases in service fees, these actions very likely served to exclude many persons who most needed help to replace their lost public support.

Income Assistance

Underlying the health, education, and social services needs of children is the family's income. Of all the recent changes in federal social policy, the AFDC changes have had the most far-reaching effects on children. Not only have families lost some or all of their benefits, but they also simultaneously lost eligibility for many other support programs, often including medicaid, employment training, day care, and other social services. The nonprofit sector generally does not provide direct income supplements, but rather offers emergency assistance in food, shelter, and so on. Government cutbacks in social spending, therefore, have fallen full force on needy children and their families.

Outlook for the Future

Although the precise effects differ across the service areas, it is clear that the government retrenchment of the early 1980s has indeed hampered the provision of human services to needy children and their families. Despite the varying strategies employed by state and local governments and by nonprofit organizations to cope with decreased federal funding, most children's services faced seriously diminished resources leading to changes in service offerings—that is, agencies tended to favor crisis assistance over prevention and basic services over specialized ones; reductions in the quantity and quality of services; and shifts in the population focus, arising from both the increased reliance on service charges and, less often, from agencies' pursuit of public dollars. One nonprofit provider of day care and other social services described how he managed to increase its government funding in this way: "While we have lost all our CETA workers and have had some other cuts [for example, Title XX], we have added new programs for Asian Americans and refugees because funds have been available for these populations."[1]

The evidence of a shift in population focus does not answer the question of how much change has occurred and what the current

---

1. From an individual agency survey form distributed in 1982 by the Nonprofit Sector Project Survey of Nonprofit Service Organizations, The Urban Institute.

population focus is for nonprofit agencies. Agencies serving children widely report changes due to government funding: 60 percent of the organizations agree that government funds have caused nonprofit organizations to direct more services to the disadvantaged, and 22 percent of children's nonprofit agencies believe that receipt of federal funds has significantly distorted the activities and objectives of their agency.

The devolution of previous federal responsibility to state and local governmental levels and to the private sector has left a significant deficit in children's services. The federal government has had a large role in ensuring the provision of human services to children, and it seems unlikely that other major sources can be found in a short period of time. Coupled with inflation, the federal cutbacks have been disastrous for many organizations. Former recipients are left to their familiar coping patterns: deferring routine care, turning to lower quality or less appropriate help, and thus facing crisis situations more often. And the situation only promises to worsen. Federal deficit projections continue to rise, and public support for social spending correspondingly continues to erode.

Where do we go from here? Which promises to our children will we keep? The problems of income, education, employment, and family functioning cannot be adequately handled piecemeal and through crisis intervention; many believe that there must be a national mandate, a service agenda to enlist the aid of both the public and the private sectors. According to this view, before government and the nonprofit sector can develop such complementary service priorities, there must be much greater awareness on the part of not only policymakers but also the general public of the needs of America's children and of the current constraints to fulfilling those needs. This book is a small step toward that goal.

APPENDIX

Primary Sources of Data

The primary data sources for this book were three studies conducted by The Urban Institute from 1981 through 1984, as described below.

1. Grant-in-Aid Study, Contract HEW-100-79-0174, sponsored by the Department of Health and Human Services, including a fiscal limitations study and a child welfare finance study.
   Problem: Developments at the federal level and within the states and localities provide the nonfederal levels of government with a unique opportunity and challenge to shape their health and human service programs. States have reacted in varying ways to the cutbacks in federal funding accompanying the creation of block grant programs and to other changes in federal social policy. This project was designed to investigate states' fiscal, programmatic, and legislative responses to federal initiatives in human services in general and in child welfare in particular, to provide systematic information useful to policymakers at all levels of government.
   Method: Using a case study methodology, the project examined human service programs in eighteen states and child welfare service programs in six states. Analysis of budgetary data on expenditure shifts was combined with interviews of individuals representing the administering agencies, the governor or local executive, and the state legislature. The study focused specifically on tracking state developments in human services through programs included in the block grants and through new or established categorical programs. Of particular interest was the delineation of the strategies developed in the states for coping with a variety of changes.
   Principal investigators: Eugene C. Durman, fiscal limitations; Madeleine H. Kimmich, child welfare.

2. Community Impact Study, sponsored by a consortium of private

foundations and corporations, under the auspices of The Urban Institute's Changing Domestic Priorities project.

Problem: Recent changes in federal social policy and budgetary commitments have been handled in many varying ways by state governments. The impact of the federal changes at the local level is difficult to predict. This study was designed to examine in detail the impact of federal changes in local communities.

Method: A team of researchers visited each of four communities— San Diego, Boston, Detroit, and Richmond, Virginia—to interview local officials, service providers, and advocates concerning the impact of federal social policy changes. Respondents commented on social services, education, employment and training programs and on budgetary, regulatory, and tax policies.

Principal investigator: Harold Wolman.

3. Nonprofit Sector Project, sponsored by a consortium of foundations; the analysis of agencies serving children and youth, by the Foundation for Child Development. Currently under the auspices of the Governance and Management Research Center at The Urban Institute.

Problem: In recent years considerable attention has been focused on the role of private voluntary organizations and how they respond to governmental retrenchment. Central questions are, can they cope with budget cuts in a period of economic stress, and do the coping strategies vary by service area, size of organization, and other organizational characteristics?

Method: To begin to understand the relation between government and nonprofit organizations, it was necessary to develop basic data on the size and scope of the sector and to monitor the behavior of individual nonprofit organizations. The Urban Institute analyzed data prepared by the Internal Revenue Service and the Bureau of the Census to derive the basic size and dimensions of the sector. It also compiled a list of nonprofit organizations in sixteen sites across the country and mailed questionaires to a sample of these service organizations. Questions focused on service delivery functions and response to government retrenchment. Analyses are currently being done for the entire sample, for each of the sixteen individual sites, and for a cross-site sample of agencies primarily serving children and youth.

Principal investigator: Lester Salamon.